*Tales of the Road*

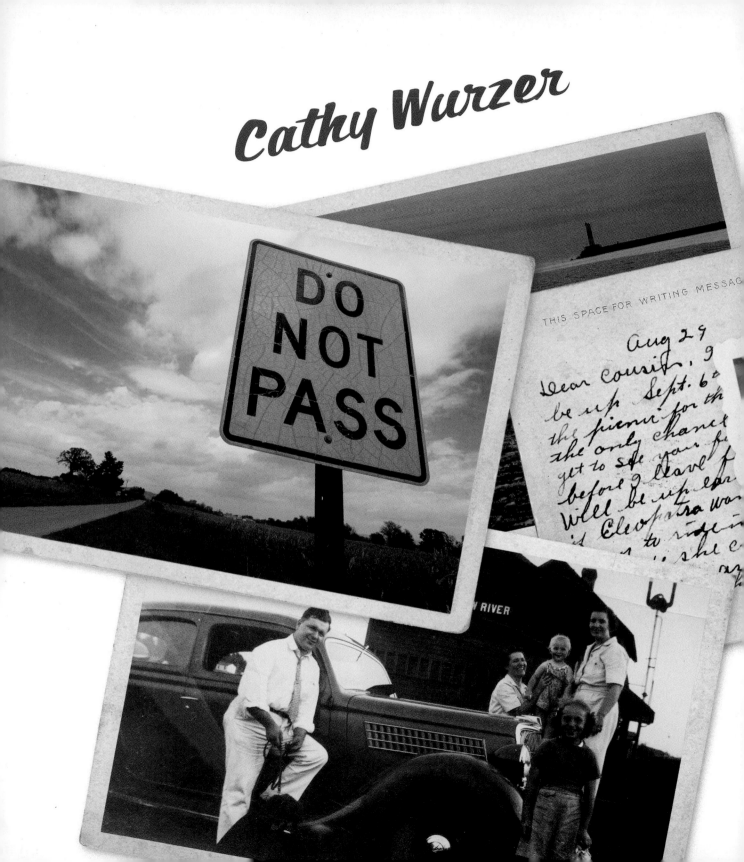

THIS SPACE FOR WRITING MESSAGES.

Tuesday
Dear Auntie Dora. We
are having simply a
marvellous tim.

POST CARD

THIS SPACE FOR A

TALES of the ROAD
Highway 61

MINNESOTA HISTORICAL SOCIETY PRESS

www.mhspress.org

The Minnesota Historical Society Press is a member of the Association of American University Presses.

Book and jacket design by Cathy Spengler Design, Minneapolis.

Manufactured in China by C&C Offset Printing Co.

10 9 8 7 6 5 4 3 2 1

♾ The paper used in this publication meets the minimum requirements of the American National Standard for Information Sciences— Permanence for Printed Library Materials, ANSI Z39.48-1984.

International Standard Book Number

ISBN: 978-0-87351-626-6 (cloth)

ISBN: 978-0-87351-829-1 (paper)

LIBRARY OF CONGRESS CATALOGING-IN-PUBLICATION DATA

Wurzer, Cathy.
  Tales of the road : Highway 61 / Cathy Wurzer.
     p. cm.
  Includes bibliographical references and index.
  ISBN-13: 978-0-87351-626-6 (cloth : alk. paper)
  ISBN-10: 0-87351-626-5 (cloth : alk. paper)
   1. Minnesota—Description and travel—
     Anecdotes.
   2. United States Highway 61—
     Description and travel—Anecdotes.
   3. Historic sites—Minnesota—Anecdotes.
   4. Historic buildings—Minnesota—Anecdotes.
   5. Minnesota— History, Local—Anecdotes.
   6. Wurzer, Cathy—Travel—Minnesota—
     Anecdotes.
   7. Minnesota—History, Local—
     Pictorial works.
   8. United States Highway 61—Pictorial works.
   9. Historic sites—Minnesota—Pictorial works.
  10. Historic buildings—Minnesota—
     Pictorial works.
   I. Minnesota Historical Society. Press.
  II. Title.

F610.W87 2008
977.6—dc22
                              2008010713

Poem on page 102 by Nell Mabey published in *Whimpie of Bramble Haw* (Falmouth Publishing House, 1955).

To the people along the highway

whose stories needed to be told

Duluth to St. Paul

Bluff Country

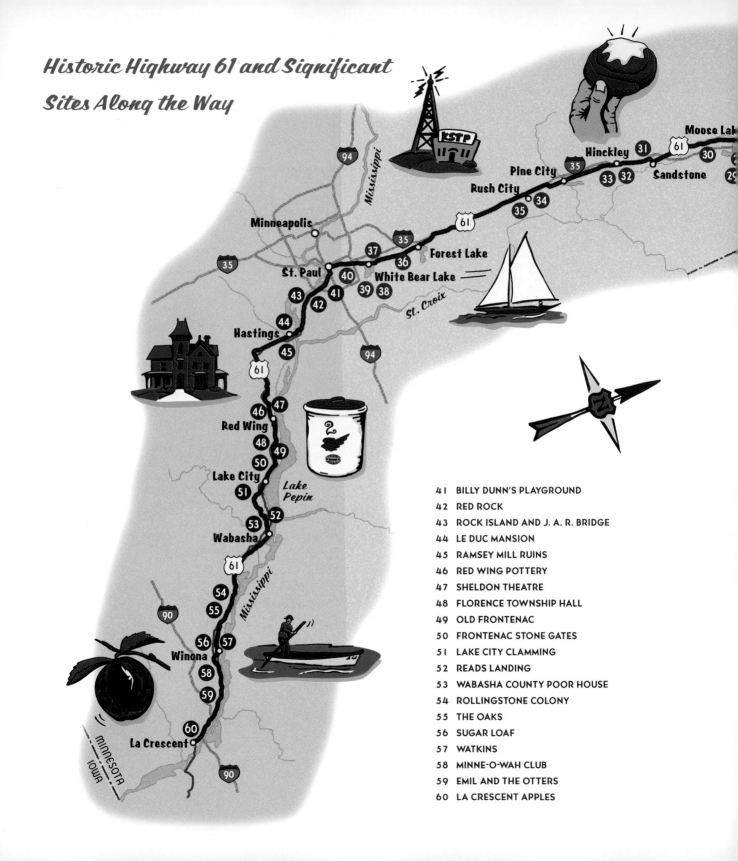

Historic Highway 61 and Significant Sites Along the Way

41 BILLY DUNN'S PLAYGROUND
42 RED ROCK
43 ROCK ISLAND AND J. A. R. BRIDGE
44 LE DUC MANSION
45 RAMSEY MILL RUINS
46 RED WING POTTERY
47 SHELDON THEATRE
48 FLORENCE TOWNSHIP HALL
49 OLD FRONTENAC
50 FRONTENAC STONE GATES
51 LAKE CITY CLAMMING
52 READS LANDING
53 WABASHA COUNTY POOR HOUSE
54 ROLLINGSTONE COLONY
55 THE OAKS
56 SUGAR LOAF
57 WATKINS
58 MINNE-O-WAH CLUB
59 EMIL AND THE OTTERS
60 LA CRESCENT APPLES

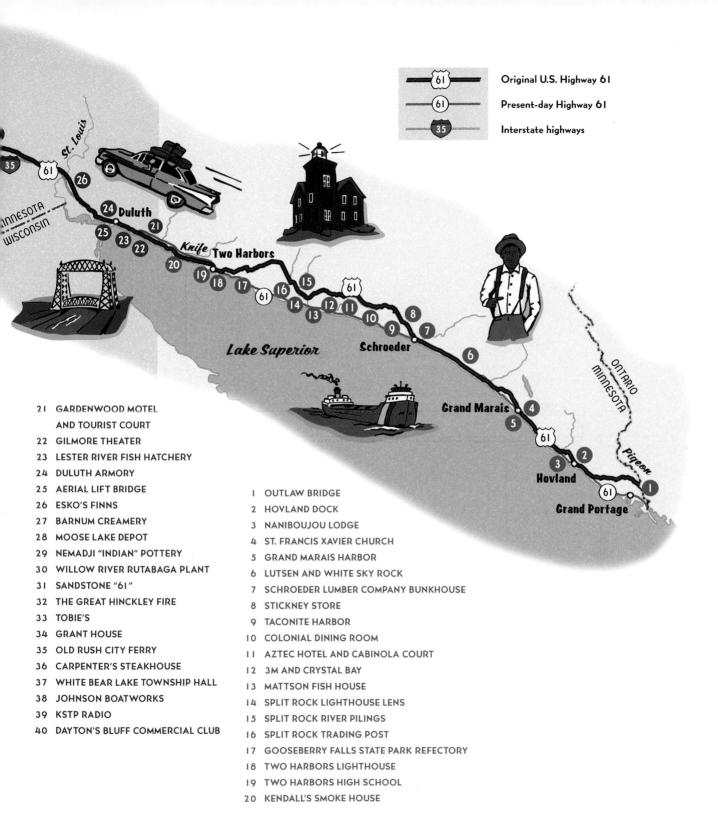

Original U.S. Highway 61

Present-day Highway 61

Interstate highways

Preface

When asked to name some of the iconic people, places, and things that symbolize Minnesota for the state's 150th birthday in 2008, many residents thought a ribbon of highway that runs from the Canadian border to the Wisconsin state line encompasses all that is Minnesota. Indeed, no other roadway tells Minnesota's story better than does Highway 61. The road, originally a footpath for native Indians, has been the source of struggle and success, tragedy and triumph. Entrepreneurs, bootleggers, and gangsters made or lost fortunes along the highway. Some even

lost their lives. Farmers, miners, fishermen, and lumberjacks scratched out a living along its route. Preachers tried to save souls. Early settlers tried to save themselves.

Highway 61 not only illuminates the state's history; it encapsulates Minnesota's natural beauty. From its start at the Pigeon River, a watery boundary with Canada, the road runs all the way down to New Orleans and the mouth of the Mississippi River, nearly seventeen hundred miles. The far northern portion of the route snakes along the shores of one of the world's largest freshwater lakes—Lake Superior—and its craggy coastline before dropping down into the farmland and bogs of eastern Minnesota. Continuing south, the road sweeps along the bluffs of the Mississippi River before passing into Wisconsin.

One of the state's original travel guides, the WPA *Guide to Minnesota,* published in 1938, lists Highway 61 as its first tour. The guide writers were among the earliest to document local history along routes like Highway 61; if not for their hard work, much of what we know about the sites and stories along the road would have been lost decades ago. In this book I've tried to share with readers stories of the places along Highway 61 that stand and beckon us—and those that have been lost to time.

I love old, abandoned buildings. There are several along this highway. Each has secrets and stories within its walls. The same may be said of people. The people and places that have shaped the history of the towns along Highway 61 have fascinating stories, but unless told they live only in the hearts and memories of those who remain. As a reporter, it has sometimes been my job—and certainly it is my passion—to tell those long-buried tales for future generations.

I don't know about you, but I'm always up for a road trip. I love driving, so let's set the odometer, buckle up, and settle in for an eventful trip down Highway 61.

Tales of the Road

Highway 61 has had many identities and configurations. Some portions of the road had their earliest beginnings as paths for Native Americans on foot or horseback. At least one section, from Wabasha to Hastings, was built by the federal government as a military road before Minnesota became a state. Almost forty years after that road was completed, in 1895, the first car was exhibited in Minnesota, and it caused quite a stir. It was only the beginning of a love affair with cars that remains to this day.

In the earliest days of automobile travel, when roads were no more than paths hacked out of the woods, drivers looked for color-coded signs to figure out where they were going. The Duluth–Twin City Highway to Port Arthur, Ontario, was known as the "Black and White Trail." The Duluth to Fargo trail was marked in green and white. The system, simple and straightforward, was put into place by automobile clubs and the American Trail Blazing Association.

Trail was a pretty accurate description of early roads because they were little more than rutted, often muddy, narrow paths of dirt or gravel. Drivers who dared venture out of the city found themselves up to their axles in mud during the spring or in clouds of dust during the summer months. The growing clamor for better roads actually started during the bicycle craze of the late 1880s. Supporters of the newfangled two-wheeled invention wanted level and safe surfaces on which to ride. The Good Roads Movement became a political force, but as cars became more popular and numerous, the push for more and better roads was

A typical road in 1917, this one between Two Harbors and Beaver Bay

taken up by businessmen, politicians, farmers, and the railroads. Railroad companies even built roads near their stations so passengers and freight could reach them. By 1916, through the lobbying efforts of the Good Roads backers, a federal law made government money available to help modernize roads across the country. It came at a good time, because automobile ownership was starting to take off. In 1909, the first year vehicles in Minnesota had to be registered, there were a little more than seven thousand motorized vehicles. By 1917, two hundred thousand were registered. One active member of the Good Roads Movement was Charles

Babcock, a merchant from Elk River who helped pass legislation that paved the way (pun intended) for Minnesota's modern trunk highway system. Babcock later became the state's first highway commissioner.

The Minnesota highway system was launched in the early 1920s, at the same time auto ownership was revving up across the country. Minnesotans were hardly left in the dust: in 1920, there were 330,000 registered vehicles in the state and that number jumped to 744,000 by 1930. The state's early web of roads and bridges—meant to link major areas—numbered some seventy routes covering more than sixty-eight hundred miles. Among those early roads were State Highways One and Three. Highway One linked St. Paul with Duluth; Highway Three connected St. Paul to La Crosse, Wisconsin; and the two met on Mounds Boulevard at Sixth Street. They were to become Highway 61.

Intense local efforts sought to open up the North Shore to tourism and trade by extending Trunk Highway One northeast from Duluth. Intrepid businessmen pushed through an early road from Canada to Duluth in 1917, dubbing it the Lake Superior International Highway—its informal name until officially christened as such amid great fanfare in 1925. Before all the celebrations, it took a lot of work—dangerous work—to create the highway, but engineers, lawmakers, and businessmen all knew the road would be key to opening up the area to tourism. The star attraction, of course, was Lake Superior.

While the original road looped through the woods several miles inland, engineers selected a lakeside route because it was much more scenic and efficient, never mind that Silver Creek Cliff, near Two Harbors, proved an immense and

Crews grading Highway 61 in downtown Hinckley, ca. 1926

expensive roadblock. Some sixty-five tons of explosives were used to blast a gash along the cliff on which to run the road. Commissioner Babcock called this stretch "probably the most expensive mile of road" in the state at the time: it cost fifty thousand dollars. The results were spectacular, if not unnerving. Drivers would carefully inch their way up and around the outside of Silver Creek Cliff because of the sheer

The author's mother's family on a road trip to Willow River, ca. 1941

drop to the lake below. Still, motorists enjoyed the beautiful—if potentially heart-stopping—scenery. The unpaved road and the bridge over the Gooseberry River opened with much hoopla in 1925. It took a few more years, until 1929, before the road was paved from Duluth south to Hastings. By 1940, the entire highway was paved.

Tourists flocked to the North Shore in droves, and the International Highway also became known as the North Shore Road. Its virtues for man and machine were poetically, if not pretentiously, touted in a 1933 publication: "You will find new pep and a zest for living to say nothing of seeing first hand the finest bit of scenery between the Katskills [*sic*] and the Rockies. Even your car will respond to the change of locality, and you will be surprised how it will want to eat up the wonderful road just because the lakeshore breezes have made the motor so extra peppy."

The North Shore Road officially became U.S. Highway 61 in 1934, as did Highway 3 from St. Paul to La Crosse. Also this year, the highway department expanded the trunk highway system and consolidated and renamed redundant state routes. The southern end of Highway 61 is also known as the Great River Road, part of the series of local and federal byways that skim the Mississippi River from Minnesota down to New Orleans.

Short stretches of the original highway alignment still exist, but you have to know where to look. The road has been revamped twice in Newport, one of the busiest sections of 61 between St. Paul and La Crosse. An original stretch of Highway 61 ex-

Abandoned alignment of Highway 61 south of Kellogg

ists as a frontage road, Hastings Avenue. Along it is the old Fritzie Fresh Candy Company and Steve's Newport Drive Inn. From there the road continues south, in fits and starts, until it reaches the old Cottage View, one of the Twin Cities' last surviving drive-in movie theaters.

A long stretch of the old two-lane highway used until 1970 survives south of the town of Kellogg and east of the modern four-lane highway. The road was widened and large swaths of towns along it were lost when Highway 61 became an expressway south of Wabasha in the 1960s and '70s. Several pieces of old U.S. 61 are under the Minnesota Department of Transportation's jurisdiction. Minnesota 361 runs for nearly six miles from Rush City to the junction of Minnesota 70, south of Pine City. A couple of miles of Minnesota 23 between Sandstone and Minnesota 18 use the old 61 route. Beyond Sandstone, Highway 61 becomes County Road 61 here and there until Duluth.

Highway 61 was a major transportation artery for little towns like Hinckley, Willow River, and Barnum. But change was quick in the 1960s and '70s when Interstate 35 came through just a few miles east of the highway. Actually, I-35 is a story unto itself, the cause of some heated exchanges in one of the most controversial of Minnesota's gubernatorial races. The election of 1962, between incumbent Republican Governor Elmer L. Andersen and Democratic challenger Karl Rolvaag, saw charges from Rolvaag supporters that the timetable for the interstate's completion was speeded up and the road's construction was shoddy. This hot-button issue became one of the pivotal stories of the election. It was a very close contest. In a recount that took nearly four and a half months, Rolvaag won by a mere ninety-one votes; the closest election in state history. The interstate went through, the concrete was durable, and the towns left behind on a less-used Highway 61 started to wither.

U.S. 61 became Minnesota 61 around 1990, but no matter its official title, most motorists feel that the route along the North Shore out of Duluth is the most iconic part of the entire road. It goes beyond being simply a means of transportation: for many, the 150 miles of Highway 61 along the North Shore is a destination. Some people remember the hairpin curves along parts of the road that got motorists' hearts beating a little faster. Some of those twists have been straightened out. Two tunnels, between Two Harbors and Silver Bay, were blasted through rocky hills in order to bypass sections that were threatening to fall into the lake—not to mention the cars and trucks that actually had. It was quite an engineering feat to drill out those tunnels in the 1990s, just as it had been to build a road along the steep cliffs of Lake Superior decades before.

No matter the alignment, configuration, or designation, Highway 61 has always meandered through some of Minnesota's most beautiful terrain. Chances are it will forever be one of the state's best-known roadways.

Highway 61 between Lake City and Wabasha

Looking down on Highway 61 from Silver Creek Cliff

Legend

🛣 **61**	Original U.S. Highway 61
🛣 **61**	Present-day Highway 61
🛣 **35**	Interstate highways

ONTARIO
MINNESOTA

Pigeon

Grand Portage

61

Brule

2 **Hovland**

3

61

4

5 **Grand Marais**

6

Lake Superior

Temperance

8 **7**
Schroeder

9

10

61

11

12

Split Rock

13

15 **14**

16

17

61

Knife

18

19 **Two Harbors**

20

1 OUTLAW BRIDGE

2 HOVLAND DOCK

3 NANIBOUJOU LODGE

4 ST. FRANCIS XAVIER CHURCH

5 GRAND MARAIS HARBOR

6 LUTSEN AND WHITE SKY ROCK

7 SCHROEDER LUMBER COMPANY BUNKHOUSE

8 STICKNEY STORE

9 TACONITE HARBOR

10 COLONIAL DINING ROOM

11 AZTEC HOTEL AND CABINOLA COURT

12 3M AND CRYSTAL BAY

13 MATTSON FISH HOUSE

14 SPLIT ROCK LIGHTHOUSE LENS

15 SPLIT ROCK RIVER PILINGS

16 SPLIT ROCK TRADING POST

17 GOOSEBERRY FALLS STATE PARK REFECTORY

18 TWO HARBORS LIGHTHOUSE

19 TWO HARBORS HIGH SCHOOL

20 KENDALL'S SMOKE HOUSE

TWO HARBORS LIGHT HOUSE

CARD

THIS SPACE FOR ADDRESS ONLY.

PLACE
STAMP HERE

DOMESTIC
ONE CENT

FOREIGN
TWO CENTS.

North
Shore

The northern end of Highway 61 is a good place to begin. What was once a bustling border crossing is now simply a wide spot in the road, the pavement cracked and studded with potholes. A faded Canadian flag waves listlessly in the breeze a river's width from where the bridge once was. A metal guardrail marks the end of the road; beyond it, a plunge, straight down, into the Pigeon River. Concrete footings cling to the cliffs on both sides of the river, the only evidence there was a bridge here, one of the very first in the area to link Minnesota with Canada.

It is quiet now at the end of the road, quiet and peaceful. A few paces off the pavement stands a solitary cabin, nestled in a thick stand of pine trees, kept company by several very old and rundown tourist cottages. Those tiny shacks are the last vestiges of the many businesses that used to operate along both sides of the river. There were cafes and gas stations, bars and resorts, and cars by the dozens. All that activity moved a few miles downstream in the 1960s, leaving behind little more than colorful memories of what was known as the "Outlaw Bridge."

In the mid-1900s, cars were becoming more popular, but there weren't many suitable places to take the novel machines. Existing roads were old stagecoach and wagon routes, rutted and virtually impassable at times. Businessmen on both sides of the border agreed that more and better roads were needed. After all, before 1915 the only way to cross the international boundary from Fort William and Port Arthur, Ontario, to Duluth was by a small chartered boat or one of the steamboat ferries that ran up and down Lake Superior.

There was a lot of pressure on politicians to do something about building a road. On the Canadian side, an old logging trail ran to the edge of the Pigeon River. While the Canadians worked on improving that bush trail, Minnesota

The original "Outlaw Bridge," with steep drop on U.S. side, 1917

officials sought to extend a road northward from Grand Marais to the river's edge. Then there was the question of linking the two roads: what to do about a bridge?

Under international treaty, the border could be permanently bridged only by joint action of the U.S. and Canadian federal governments. Businessmen from Port Arthur and Fort William, Ontario, and Duluth and Grand Marais, Minnesota, all agreed formal approval would take too long. The Rotary clubs on both sides of the border met and cooked up a scheme to build their own bridge. About one year and almost five thousand dollars later, the wooden bridge was finished. Well, very nearly finished. The approaches on both ends of the span were a little short and steep, more so on the U.S. side, because the donated lumber had run out. However, according to a story in the May 2, 1917, *Cook County News Herald,* the bridge was deemed to be safe and more than usable. In fact, a gentleman named Emil Hall was the first American to cross the bridge in his 1917 Ford, and he reported no problems.

A grand opening was held on August 18, a gala affair, the bridge freshly painted white and decorated for the occasion. Twin parades of festively adorned cars left their respective towns with great fanfare. The Canadians were a bit more prepared, accompanied by a pipe band and a mobile motor and tire repair shop. About five hundred people attended the ceremonies. The sign over the bridge that day read "Pigeon River Bridge–International Boundary," but because it was built without formal government approval, it became better known as the Outlaw Bridge. Looking ahead to the 1930s, that name would prove prophetic, indeed.

The bridge was immediately popular, and almost overnight businesses appeared on either side of the crossing, along with customs agents and border patrol officers. Ed and Mabel Ryden owned the Pigeon River Resort, managing twenty-three cabins. In an oral history for the Cook County Historical Society, the Rydens recalled that the bridge closed at 11 PM and opened the next morning at 7 AM. If some unfortunate motorist didn't make it over in time, he'd have to spend the night. The Rydens charged $2.50 for lodging. If visitors arrived late, they took a key, found an empty cabin, and paid in the morning.

The Pigeon River crossing could be a pretty raucous place. There was no shortage of establishments where a motorist could order a drink and something to eat. The drinking got many people into trouble, especially during Prohibition. Canada didn't have a ban on alcohol during the 1930s, while the United States did. That law didn't stop Americans (or Canadians) from attempting to smuggle alcohol across the border—and thus the Outlaw Bridge lived up to its name. Customs officials were pretty wily: if they caught a motorist with bottles of alcohol, they made use of the "crying rock," a boulder on which agents would smash illegal bottles of booze, oftentimes in front of the chagrined motorist.

Footings from the international border bridge that once spanned the Pigeon River

Darrel and Larry Ryden, in an interview with the Cook County Historical Society, remembered that once a year Canadian customs officials would destroy all the confiscated liquor, beer, and cigarettes by throwing them off the bridge into the Pigeon River. Larry reported, "We were down there picking it up as fast as they were throwing it over." The enterprising brothers then sold the undamaged cans of beer to tourists for fifteen cents each.

After many years, the wooden bridge became pretty rickety, and there were some bad accidents. At least one car broke through the wooden railing and plunged into the river, spurring calls for a new, safer bridge. In 1930, the old wooden bridge came down and in its place rose a steel truss bridge that remained through the mid-1960s. Until this point, U.S. Highway 61 had run inland from the Pigeon River to Hovland, bypassing Grand Portage. In the 1960s, a new stretch of highway was built through Grand Portage, including a new border crossing about six miles downstream. The crossing opened in 1964 and now handles as many as three hundred thousand vehicles a year—traffic levels the old Outlaw Bridge's builders would never have dreamed possible. No doubt they also never imagined how successful their renegade venture would become.

THE POET IN THE WOODS

I've been a reporter for a long time, and I have met some of the most interesting people in the strangest of places. My pilgrimage to the site of the old Outlaw Bridge in the middle of the Grand Portage Indian Reservation included a meeting I would have never imagined.

One September afternoon in 2007, my photographer and I were trying to find what remains of the original Highway 61 and the footings of the old bridge linking Minnesota to Canada over the Pigeon River. We didn't have the best directions, and my confidence that we would find the border crossing was starting to wane along with the late afternoon sun. We weren't sure where we were as we drove deeper into an already remote area of the reservation—and then we spotted a rusted street sign that read "Old Highway 61." After nearly twenty minutes of bumping down the abandoned highway, we finally found ourselves in a clearing, but, lacking the telltale signs of a customs office or guard shack or any of the other buildings that once lined the road, we couldn't be certain if it was the old border crossing.

We noticed a tiny cabin tucked into the woods. I wasn't happy about knocking on some strange door in the middle of the wilderness, but as we walked up the path, of all things, Minnesota Public Radio's program The Splendid Table was blaring from the little cabin. The door was answered by an older, tiny slip of a woman: we had stumbled into the backyard of noted poet and essayist Joanne Hart. I'm not sure who was more surprised to meet the other—Joanne or yours truly. Joanne is in her eighties, vibrant and vigorous and still writing. She lives a simple life without many modern conveniences in the deserted village that indeed used to be the old border crossing.

Joanne was quite interested in our project and knows a thing or two about writing, having published several books reflecting on life among her Ojibwe neighbors, including Witch Tree, I Walk on the River at Dawn, In These Hills, and The Village Schoolmaster. What a treat to meet such an accomplished and charming woman in the middle of nowhere. Well, to an outsider it may be "nowhere," but to Joanne Hart it is her beloved home where she finds inspiration and a special magic that brings her poetry to life.

HOVLAND DOCK

The mammoth cement dock that juts into Lake Superior near Hovland has seen better days. The end of it broke off and cascaded into the lake years ago.

The Hovland dock, originally constructed of wood, dates back to 1902. The cement version was built in 1918. The dock was one of several along the North Shore, each of them serving as a kind of supply depot for their respective communities. The Hovland dock was a key portal where goods of all kinds, passengers, and the U.S. mail were loaded and unloaded from a fleet of ferries that made regular runs up and down the shore to Duluth.

Why ferries? Travel in the early 1900s was difficult to say the least. The "roads" settlers used actually followed ancient Indian trails between Grand Portage and Duluth. They were terribly rutted and nearly impassable at certain times of the year. While companies like the Duluth and Iron Range Railroad operated inland, people along the North Shore had to travel a long way to catch a train. Some of the ferries on Lake Superior were owned by large railroad companies. James J. Hill's Great Northern Railroad managed the *Northwest* and the *Northland*. There were other ferries, but the best known was the *America*.

Hovland dock

She was built in Detroit in 1898 and began her trips up and down the shore in 1902, the same year the Hovland dock was built. The *America* was an elegant steamer, with staterooms and sleeping accommodations, "carpeted stairs and mirrored halls." She carried passengers, barrels of fish caught by area fishermen, groceries and other supplies, and the mail three times a week between Duluth, Ontario's Port Arthur (known today as Thunder Bay), and the resort area of Isle Royale, with stops in Tofte, Hovland, and Grand Portage. People in smaller North Shore communities waited until they heard the *America*'s whistle and then rowed out to meet her with their fish catch or, in the case of Matilda Tormondsen's father, the mail. William Clarence Smith (known to everyone as W.C.) was the postmaster at Schroeder. In a 2007 article for the *Schroeder Area Historical Society Newsletter,* Matilda remembered, "A rope ladder was let down from the gangway [of the *America*], and passengers, freight and mail were delivered this way into a skiff which was six feet below." This delivery method could pose a problem if there were high seas on the lake, not an uncommon occurrence.

Steamer America*, ca. 1905*

The *America* and similar steamers were one of the major links to civilization for people along the North Shore until Highway 61 was completed in the mid-1920s. People could make the trek inland and catch the train, but the steamers were more convenient. It was a twist of fate, then, when the *America* sank near Isle Royale in 1928, just a few years after the highway became the main transportation artery for the North Shore. Today, the *America*'s remains are visible just a couple of feet below the water's surface off Isle Royale National Park. She's a popular spot for scuba divers, who like to explore her submerged deck, the galley, and her once elegant rooms.

In Hovland during the summer and fall, amateur scuba divers paddle around the old cement dock and, on good days, retrieve small bottles or other trinkets. They appear to have been thrown overboard by passengers, perhaps even those on the *America*.

NANIBOUJOU LODGE

The great beauty of the North Shore has attracted untold numbers of admirers, and if it hadn't been for the stock market crash of 1929, some of those visitors might have included the likes of baseball great Babe Ruth and boxing champ Jack Dempsey. Ruth, Dempsey, and other wealthy notables were charter members of the exclusive Naniboujou Club, located about fifteen miles out of Grand Marais.

Named for a Cree Indian deity of the woods, the Naniboujou Club was intended to be the private playground for a select group of wealthy investors. Plans for the enterprise were unveiled in March 1928 by the Naniboujou Holding Company, which had obtained more than three thousand acres of land along the North Shore and the Brule River. There would be a clubhouse with a dining room, 150 sleeping rooms, a golf course, and tennis courts. Membership was open to the friends—and the friends of friends—of the twenty-four-member Board of Governors.

Naniboujou Club aerial view, ca. 1940

A grand celebration was held on July 7, 1929, to christen the new lodge. Governor Theodore Christianson was invited, as were other well-known and well-to-do individuals. Those in attendance may well have done the very same thing most of today's visitors do when entering the lodge: stand and stare.

The Naniboujou Club's founders had hired French artist Antoine Goufee to paint the rectangular room with its twenty-foot-high ceiling. The results are breathtaking. The vivid Cree Indian designs, with their Art Deco feel, make the dining room one of the most eye-catching spaces in the state. Some have called Naniboujou's distinctive interior "the north woods' answer to the Sistine Chapel." No one seems to know why Goufee decided to interpret Cree designs, but the re-

The lodge's stunning dining room

sult is certainly memorable. And, as if the riot of color on the walls and ceiling isn't enough, rising up at one end of the room is an imposing stone fireplace, said to be one of the state's largest, constructed with two hundred tons of native rock.

In this elegant atmosphere, the newly formed Naniboujou Holding Company's club began entertaining members. Then, just three months after the initial celebration, disaster struck with the stock market crash of October 29, 1929. The club fell on hard times, as did the rest of the country. Instead of touting itself as an exclusive enclave, to stay afloat the club began soliciting the general public for memberships. Despite these efforts, by 1935 the club was in foreclosure. Hotelier Arthur Roberts— who had a hand in building the Pine Beach Hotel on Gull Lake, which later became Madden's Resort—bought Naniboujou in 1939, and the lodge has had several owners since.

What hasn't changed is the interior of the dining area, which has never been touched in any manner since Antoine Goufee completed the vivid designs in 1929. The current owners haven't even cleaned the walls, deciding that leaving the historic paintings alone is the best option. The guest list may not be as lofty as it was in 1929, but the Naniboujou Lodge remains a popular spot for tourists and a historic landmark along Highway 61.

The split log walls of the tiny St. Francis Xavier Church contain the joys, the sorrows, and the hopes of generations. It is located in what was known as Chippewa City, a village about a mile east of Grand Marais.

Many of its parishioners walked two paths: that of their ancestry, Anishinaabe or Ojibwe, and that as members of the Catholic church. The church was the focal point of the village, and it looks much the same as it did when Jesuit missionaries established it in 1895. When the Jesuits arrived with a goal of saving souls, they found a village of about one hundred families, mostly Ojibwe people who had been living in Grand Marais, including John Beargrease, a well-known mail carrier who made winter runs from Two Harbors to Grand Marais via dogsled.

The Chippewa City community also included the Morrison family. James Morrison, Sr., was one of the elders of the St. Francis Xavier Church. Before the church was built, Morrison would sometimes hold Mass in his home and officiate if a priest wasn't available. His grandson, the nationally noted artist George Morrison, wrote in his 1998 book *Turning the Feather Around* that his grandfather "usually sat in a gray pulpit chair he had built. The chair was always located to the left of the church door where he greeted people and officiated as the bell ringer. . . . When I stand on Chippewa Beach and look up to see the church, it is the only remnant of my grandfather." In 2000, George Morrison was buried out of the Chippewa City church, a church his grandfather helped found.

The Benedictine priests of St. John's Abbey in Collegeville took over St. Francis Xavier from the Jesuit missionaries in 1905. They sent Father Simon Lampe to run the Indian mission, establish another church in Grand Marais, and attend the needs of souls in Grand Portage. Father Simon lived in a small room behind the altar at St. Francis Xavier. But as the population of Chippewa City dwindled, so did church membership.

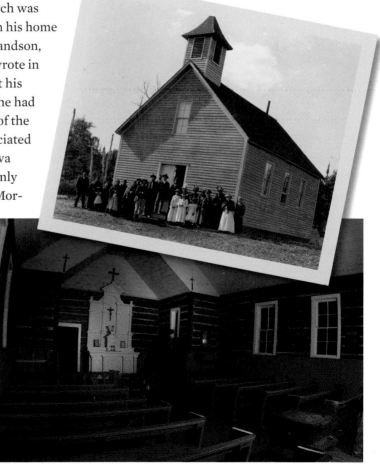

top: St. Francis Xavier Church, ca. 1900

bottom: The old church is open for tours during the summer.

The last Mass was said on Christmas 1936, with only one or two families in the wooden pews.

The church's graveyard is across the highway, which decades ago looked far different than it does today. Many burial plots had wooden "spirit houses" over them, a traditional Ojibwe way of marking a grave. Family members might put offerings at the spirit house's door as a way to keep the departed soul happy, so that it could continue peacefully on its spiritual journey. Large wooden crosses were also erected, but they didn't last. Some of the graves' original locations were lost after a major cleanup of the cemetery in the late 1950s. The church itself was empty for many years until 1998, when the Catholic Diocese of Duluth donated it to the Cook County Historical Society for use as a museum.

Highway 61 cuts through what was the village of Chippewa City. But the St. Francis Xavier Church still serves as an important cultural milepost in the area. As George Morrison put it, "The church remains a symbol of our community and our life there."

GRAND MARAIS HARBOR

Grand Marais has been a fur trading post, a fishing village, and a logging town. Today, this picturesque lakeside village is a prime tourist destination. One of the most photographed sites in Grand Marais has to be the harbor.

Ancient lava flows weathered unevenly to create the distinctive double harbor. To the east, it is enclosed by a wide gravel bar created by debris shoved together by hundreds of years of pounding waves. The Ojibwe, the area's original residents,

THE ANNUAL FISHERMEN'S PICNIC IN GRAND MARAIS IS ONE OF THE OLDEST ON-GOING CELEBRATIONS ON THE NORTH SHORE. THE FIRST "MODERN-DAY" PICNIC WAS IN 1928.

Grand Marais Harbor

named it *Kitchi-bi-to-tig* or "double harbor" and also *Gitch-be-to-beek* or "big pond." Both were accurate descriptions. French fur trappers called it *Grand Marais* or "great marsh" because of a swamp located at the head of the bay and harbor.

The harbor has always been important to the region. When European settlers descended upon northeastern Minnesota in the 1870s, ships were needed to get supplies in to and out of the fledgling town. Despite the natural harbors, there was a push to build breakwaters and a lighthouse after the sixty-foot schooner the *Stranger* sank in a typically fierce Lake Superior storm in 1875. The original lighthouse, the first on the North Shore, was built in 1885. Crews had constructed the east breakwater just a year earlier, and the west breakwater was finished in 1901. A newer lighthouse was built in 1922, and the U.S. Coast Guard continues to use the harbor as a station, as it has since 1928.

The Grand Marais harbor has been a busy place since the first settlers appeared. Supply ships, passenger ferries, and commercial fishing boats have used the harbor, and until 1972 it was the launch site for log rafts, where thousands of cords of pulpwood were corralled and towed across the lake to paper mills. After decades of hard work, the harbor now shelters pleasure boats and plays host to admirers of its timeless beauty.

LUTSEN AND WHITE SKY ROCK

When people think of skiing in Minnesota, many think of Lutsen, where one of the North Shore's oldest resorts and some of the state's tallest peaks are located. Lutsen gained international attention during the 1976 Winter Olympics in Innsbruck, Austria, when a blond, apple-cheeked skier named Cindy Nelson sped down a mountain to win a bronze medal in the Alpine skiing competition. Cindy grew up skiing the hills of Lutsen. Her father, George Nelson, took advantage of area topography in 1948 when he opened the first and highest ski hill in Minnesota. Reaching more than one thousand feet from the base of the mountain to the peak, it became Cindy's backyard training facility.

It wasn't skiing that brought the Nelson family to the land that fronts Lake Superior, however. It was fishing. C. A. A.

Lutsen Resort, ca. 1950

(Charles) Nelson was an immigrant from Sweden who settled along the shore in the mid-1880s to fish and do some trapping and logging. C. A. A. decided to stake his claim at the mouth of the Poplar River, and if not for the help of another local family, George Nelson may never have had the chance to establish the famed Lutsen Resort.

The Poplar was a popular route into the nearby forest for a small community of Native Americans, members of the Grand Portage Band of Anishinaabe or Ojibwe people. They were led by *O je meke shig,* who was also known as Jim Gesick and who befriended his new neighbor, a fortunate turn of events for the Nelsons. Gesick and his family shared with the settlers their winter cache of food and their knowledge of the area: where the best berries were, which routes led to the choicest fishing spots, how to tap trees for maple syrup. The Nelsons' transition into their new home was helped, in part, by their Native friends. As the newcomers began to thrive, C. A. A.'s original homestead cabin was added on to, little by little, to accommodate his growing family as well as folks who found Nelson's place a convenient stop as they traveled up and down the Lake Superior shore. Nelson called his homestead "Lutsen," and it began to attract visitors who stayed to hunt and fish. Sometimes the Nelson children had to give up their beds for arriving guests. As C. A. A. Nelson played host to an increasing number of tourists, the series of white, wood-frame buildings eventually made way for a grand rustic log lodge designed by noted architect Edwin Lunde.

Conservation officer White Sky, ca. 1909

Jim Gesick and his family remained friends with the Nelsons, helping supply the burgeoning resort with moose and deer meat. One of Jim's sons, *Wah se gi jig* or White Sky, grew up with the Nelson boys. Together they attended school, hunted the woods, and fished the shoreline. White Sky became the first Native American conservation officer in the Lutsen area. Sadly, in 1913 he died from tuberculosis at age twenty-four. Carl Nelson, one of C. A. A.'s sons, named a breathtaking overlook in the hills above Caribou Lake after his friend, a fitting memorial because White Sky once had a hunting shack in those hills. Over the years, countless hikers have huffed and puffed their way up the steep cliff to White Sky Rock and been rewarded with the same panoramic view White Sky himself no doubt enjoyed.

The Lutsen resort continues to thrive. In 1988 the Nelson family sold it to another Minnesota family, and it remains one of the premier resorts along the North Shore. The descendents of Jim Gesick and White Sky continue to live in northeastern Minnesota as well, proud of their past and the quiet role their family played in a piece of North Shore history.

It isn't unusual to see tourists on the Cross River Bridge in tiny Schroeder, their cameras aimed at the rushing falls. The cascade is tough to miss, running fairly close to the highway as it plunges down the gorge, under the bridge, and out into Lake Superior.

On close inspection, cracked boulders near the Cross River may be visible, evidence of dynamiting that took place around 1895, when the Schroeder Lumber Company of Milwaukee, Wisconsin, started its logging operations here. In its time, the Schroeder Lumber Company, owned by German-born John Schroeder, was one of the country's largest lumber retailers. The company owned and operated every step in the lumber-making process, from cutting the trees, to shipping the logs, to milling them into all manner of wood products. John Schroeder managed lumber holdings throughout Lake and Cook counties in Minnesota, and his crews cut thousands of acres of trees across Michigan's Upper Peninsula and throughout northern Wisconsin.

The Cross River area was blessed with large stands of magnificent white pines, along with spruce and balsam, all of which were attractive to a firm like Schroeder's. But getting those trees cut and transported out of the woods was a tough and dangerous job.

The Schroeder Company set up a logging camp on land that is now Lamb's Resort, close to the banks of the Cross River. The large, weathered log building that present-day guests see on

Photograph of the bunkhouse sent to Horace Stickney by the Schroeder Lumber Company as proof of the land and buildings he purchased, ca. 1921

The bunkhouse, a remnant of the North Shore's largest logging operation, was listed in the National Register of Historic Places in 1986.

the resort property was a bunkhouse, the last remnant of the lumber company's presence in the region. A typical logging camp bunkhouse could shelter as many as one hundred men, but it isn't clear just how many slept in the structure that remains on the Lamb property. Usually there were rows of wooden bunk beds with hay, straw, or evergreen boughs for mattresses and straw-filled grain sacks for pillows. Cedar chips, said to keep away lice and ticks, were strewn on the floor. Bunkhouses no doubt had a distinctive smell. *Ripe* would be a good word to describe the odor of wet woolen clothes hung to dry and sweaty workers living in close quarters.

According to Mary T. Bell in *Cutting Across Time,* the Schroeder Lumber Company at Cross River had a reputation for decent living conditions, fair wages, and good food. Food was important. Lumberjacks ate a lot and ate it fast, and if the grub wasn't up to snuff, men would seek employment elsewhere. At two dollars a day, cooks in a logging camp were paid more than most, but they earned their keep, working as many as fifteen hours a day to keep everyone fed and happy.

Cutting the trees was just one part of the job; getting the logs to a sawmill was quite another. Schroeder Lumber Company loggers dynamited the top twenty feet of the Cross River waterfall in order to widen the river to facilitate the flow of logs down the channel come spring. They also built a series of dams so water could be held in reserve. Those dams would be opened, one by one, to send an adequate amount of water to keep the logs moving along the river and out into Lake Superior. Old-timers who remembered the log drives, as they were called, said the sound was deafening as the logs came crashing down the river.

Log drives were very dangerous for the men whose job was to steer the logs and keep them from jamming. These men were called "cats on logs," and, indeed, they had to be nimble as a cat to keep the logs moving in the rushing water. Often the logs would jam, and the men had to be quick to jump to safety when the jam broke apart, or they could lose their lives. Once the logs made it down the river, they were corralled into a "holding boom" that kept them from floating out into Lake Superior. The logs would remain in these booms until they could be transported across the lake.

The Schroeder Company ceased logging at the Cross River in 1905, and the crews left to log the Apostle Islands. John Schroeder died three years later. His sons ran the business for several decades after that, but in 1939 the Schroeder Lumber Company's many holdings and its well-known Milwaukee lumberyard were liquidated. Back in Minnesota, the town of Schroeder was organized in 1904, named in honor of John Schroeder, the man who helped put the area on the map with his logging operations. However, the Native American name for the area also seems fitting: the Ojibwe called it *Tchibaiatigo zibi,* which means "Spirit of Wood of the Soul River."

FATHER BARAGA'S CROSS AT THE MOUTH OF THE CROSS RIVER IS A GRANITE MARKER ON THE SITE OF THE ORIGINAL WOODEN CROSS ERECTED BY A CATHOLIC MISSIONARY IN THANKSGIVING FOR HIS SAFE PASSAGE ACROSS THE LAKE DURING A STORM IN 1846.

Many buildings along Highway 61 have had multiple lives.

Today, the handsome gray-shingled building that fronts Highway 61 in Schroeder is the keeper of many memories; appropriately enough, it is the Cross River Heritage Center and home to the Schroeder Area Historical Society. However, the building used to be a grocery store and restaurant, built by Horace Stickney and his wife, Nell. Mr. Stickney had good timing and excellent business sense.

It was the early 1920s. Horace had just bought land along the Cross River that had been logged by the Schroeder Lumber Company. Horace's background was in

Stickney Store, ca. 1929

Horace and Nell Stickney, ca. 1940

farming, but he thought this parcel was the worst farmland he had ever seen—claims made by the lumber company notwithstanding. Perhaps, he told his family, it held possibilities for something else.

The region was just beginning to attract the interest of tourists. The North Shore Highway (Highway 61) opened in 1925. Horace and his wife decided to build a small store that sold supplies to locals and tourists. They included a dining room overlooking the lovely falls of the Cross River. The Stickney Store quickly became a hub for the growing town of Schroeder. Then, disaster hit. In the fall of 1928, a gas stove in the restaurant's kitchen blew up, burning the place to the ground.

It turned out to be a small setback. Horace rebuilt and reopened the store in 1929—just in time for the historic stock market crash and the ensuing Great Depression. Things weren't looking good for the little store and its owners, until the phone company came through with crews to put up poles and string telephone lines. Horace won the contract to house and feed the twenty-five-member crews, and, little by little, the Stickneys continued to pay their bills and started to turn things around.

During the 1930s, Stickney's nephew, Harry Lamb, helped his uncle build small cabins along the Cross River and out onto the shores of Lake Superior. Despite the poor economic conditions of the 1930s, people still managed to find the money and time to escape to the North Shore. The region became a haven for hay fever sufferers because of its clean, pollen-free air.

The Stickney Store building now houses the Cross River Heritage Center.

Residents called the visitors, many of whom stayed for several weeks at a time, "hayfever-ites." There was certainly no shortage of places to stay. According to an article in the October 18, 1934, edition of the *Two Harbors Chronicle,* there were 557 resorts in the Arrowhead region and by 1935 it was expected that the number would top six hundred. The Stickney Resort was in good company.

Eventually, the Stickney Resort became known as Lamb's Resort after Harry Lamb purchased it from his uncle. It remains today, still in the hands of the Lamb family: a slice of the old North Shore, with original cabins and a breathtaking view of Lake Superior. And the Cross River Heritage Center continues to welcome visitors to Schroeder, just as the Stickney Store and restaurant did decades ago.

TACONITE HARBOR

There is a genuine ghost town along Highway 61 between Schroeder and Little Marais. Most people miss it.

To the average visitor, Taconite Harbor looks like a large field filled with tall grasses and brush. Those with sharp eyes may notice the rusting street lamp that stands like a lonely sentinel along a short strip of pothole-studded pavement. An abandoned basketball court is hidden in a thicket of trees. There are chunks of concrete curb and a couple of old manhole covers. Visitors on the access

Street scene, Taconite Harbor, ca. 1958, complete with cloud of taconite dust in the distance

road into Taconite Harbor wouldn't notice these things; they are usually on their way to the nearby boat launch on Lake Superior.

But in the late 1950s and throughout the 1960s and '70s, this community was a busy little place. The Erie Mining Company built it to house workers employed at a specially designed shipping facility on Lake Superior. Erie Mining ran taconite trains from its production plant at Hoyt Lakes to the Taconite Harbor docks, where the pellets were loaded onto ore boats and sent across the Great Lakes. The Taconite Harbor docks were designed to be some of the fastest loading facilities in the world. Freighters could be filled with tons of taconite in less than an hour and forty-five minutes. Each year, Taconite Harbor shipped out an average of 10 to 11 million tons of taconite pellets.

Twenty-four families lived in modest ranch-style homes that neatly lined the few streets of Taconite Harbor. There was a power plant, a town hall, a fire hall, a ball field, and a basketball court. For $400 down and $110 a month, many of the young couples in Taconite Harbor bought their first homes and started to raise families. This self-sufficient little village had as its focus the lifeblood of

A long-deserted basketball court at Taconite Harbor

the Iron Range: taconite. When the trains rolled in from the range to dump their load of taconite pellets into storage bins or when the long chutes of the loading dock were lowered into the ore boat holds, huge clouds of red dust billowed at the far edge of town. Women who had hung their wash outside to dry ran to pluck the items off the clothesline before they could be dirtied by the dust.

Taconite Harbor was definitely a company town. But a downturn in the taconite industry in the 1980s brought hard times. Erie Mining (then known as LTV Steel) struggled, as did other Iron Range taconite plants. Shipments to the Taconite Harbor docks dwindled. The power plant closed, and workers lost their jobs. Eventually, the mining company bought up the houses and the families moved away. Efforts were made to save the town, to no avail.

It was eerie to drive through Taconite Harbor at the end of its life and see the few remaining homes boarded up. Others were lifted from their foundations and moved away; only the concrete steps remained. Folks who lived there say they can still remember how it looked and what it was like to hear the kids playing on the basketball court, the taconite trains rumbling in the background. Interpretive displays at the nearby boat launch and up the road, at the Cross River Heritage Center in Schroeder, detail the short history of Taconite Harbor—one of the North Shore's little-known ghost towns.

COLONIAL DINING ROOM

Colonial Inn, ca. 1948

It must have seemed odd, given the rustic nature of the North Shore, to find on Highway 61 an elegant, white clapboard restaurant that looked for all the world as if it belonged in colonial Williamsburg, Virginia. The distinctive, custom-made green shutters added to the overall effect of the Colonial Dining Room as it proudly stood along the highway in Little Marais.

Colonial Inn dining room; lamp at left from Evelyn Rudstrom's collection

The Colonial began as a rough-hewn log store, built by Leonard and Evelyn Rudstrom. It was their dream to own a country store, and they loved the North Shore; thus, the Little Marais Store was established in 1935. One gas pump outside; groceries and a few rooms for tourists inside.

As more and more tourists found their way up the shore in the 1930s, the Rudstroms discovered they had to adjust their offerings to meet the demand for places to eat and stay. They added a dining room, more guest rooms, and small housekeep-

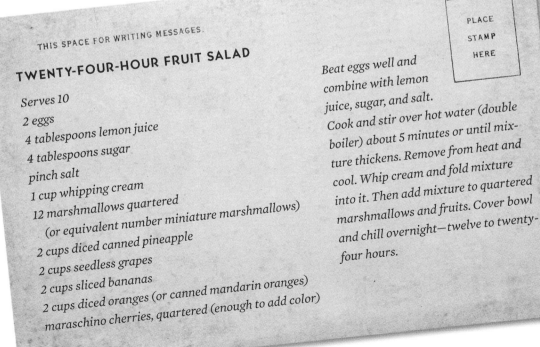

THIS SPACE FOR WRITING MESSAGES.

TWENTY-FOUR-HOUR FRUIT SALAD

Serves 10

2 eggs
4 tablespoons lemon juice
4 tablespoons sugar
pinch salt
1 cup whipping cream
12 marshmallows quartered
(or equivalent number miniature marshmallows)
2 cups diced canned pineapple
2 cups seedless grapes
2 cups sliced bananas
2 cups diced oranges (or canned mandarin oranges)
maraschino cherries, quartered (enough to add color)

Beat eggs well and combine with lemon juice, sugar, and salt. Cook and stir over hot water (double boiler) about 5 minutes or until mixture thickens. Remove from heat and cool. Whip cream and fold mixture into it. Then add mixture to quartered marshmallows and fruits. Cover bowl and chill overnight—twelve to twenty-four hours.

PLACE
STAMP
HERE

Colonial Inn building

ing cottages along the lakeshore. The business became known as the Little Marais Lodge and Store.

The transformation into a New England–style inn occurred after World War II, when the family returned to Minnesota after a couple years' absence, during which Leonard served as a mining engineer in upstate New York. While there, Evelyn started collecting antiques, and these treasures were brought back to Little Marais. The log lodge was paneled over and painted white. Inside, historic maps graced the inn and dining room walls. There were antique lamps, along with specially made shelves to hold Evelyn's impressive china collection.

Her goal was to create a fine dining experience on the North Shore, complete with Irish linens, Haviland china, and good silverware on the tables; fresh lilacs, peonies, and roses from her garden; and finger bowls that were passed at the end of each meal. It was a grand place, and guests came from all over the Midwest, many driving north from Duluth for one of the Rudstroms' sumptuous meals.

To this day, older couples who remember eating at the Colonial Dining Room or honeymooning at the lodge will stop by the store next door and ask about the old building. The resort operated continuously until 1973, and it was sold the following year, after Evelyn Rudstrom died. The Colonial Dining Room and Inn still fronts the highway, but it's empty now and in disrepair. The next-door store, which the Rudstroms built in the 1950s, is still in use. The current owners say that nostalgic visitors often ask if they can buy one of the green shutters, which are now peeling and worn. The requests are always politely declined, and what remains is a slowly fading piece of the North Shore's elegant history.

AZTEC HOTEL AND CABINOLA COURT

The North Shore towns along Highway 61 were full of people with big dreams and big ideas. Count Rudy Illgen among that number.

Between 1924 and the early 1950s, Rudy, a German immigrant who arrived in the United States in 1908, along with his wife, Mary, a native of Wadena, Minnesota, presided over a unique tourist draw: the Aztec Hotel and Cabinola Court, one of the more memorable places to stay on the North Shore.

Here's the story. In 1924, with word that a new highway would be built close to the Lake Superior shore, Rudy Illgen went looking for land. He talked with an official from the Minnesota Mining and Manufacturing Company (today's 3M). The company had abandoned operations at its nearby Crystal Bay plant several years earlier, and Rudy struck a deal to buy forty acres that were destined to be near the new highway.

According to a memoir written by his daughter Pauline, bankers in Two Harbors laughed at Rudy when he told them he wanted to build a hotel in the woods, and they refused to accept his property as collateral for a loan. The Illgens broke ground anyway and built the hotel by themselves: sawing the lumber and doing their own wiring, plumbing, plastering, and bricklaying. The hotel was patterned after an Aztec temple, inspired by the time Rudy spent in Mexico as a young man, when he took a fancy to the ancient buildings created by Aztec and Mayan Indi-

Highway 61's current alignment runs through the former site of the Cabinola Court (ca. 1935).

ans. The hotel had a dozen rooms, a dining room, a large lobby, and a magnificent hand-carved mahogany bar some fifty feet long. There was no electricity in the area until 1937, but the Aztec Hotel had lights—generated by a Mack truck motor that Rudy rigged up into his own little power plant.

During the difficult early years of the Depression, the Aztec didn't see many tourists. The guests were hunters, or fishermen, or men working on road crews or putting in local telephone lines. The Illgens charged a dollar a day for a room and meals or five dollars for the week.

A surviving cabinola, this one dubbed "Kentucky," one of thirty named after states

Pauline Illgen Petersen remembered that her father was always dreaming up ways to make extra money. One inspiration was to screen movies in the hotel. Rudy bought a movie projector and signed a contract with Columbia Pictures to show a certain number of films each year. He brought in a big screen and 150 folding chairs, and every two weeks they'd show a silent movie, the music provided by Pauline and her sister on an old player piano.

When the tourists started coming in the late 1930s, Rudy had yet another idea: he would offer small cabins that were easily accessible to the motoring public. Across the highway from the Aztec, and right next to a cliff overlook-

ing Lake Superior, Rudy built a couple dozen unique structures. They looked like tiny Quonset huts; he called them *cabinolas* and patented the design. Each was named for a state in the Union. Rudy planned to build one for each of the forty-eight states, but he managed to complete only thirty.

The tiny cabinola bathrooms are barely big enough for one person.

The Aztec Hotel and the Cabinola Court closed down during World War II. With no travel due to gasoline rationing and no help to run his tourist empire, Rudy had no option but to let the weeds grow up around the place. After the war, in 1945, Pauline and her husband worked to get the cabinolas back in shape, and business that first year was fantastic. The diminutive cabins were big enough for one bed and a postage stamp–sized bathroom, but they were what North Shore tourists of the era wanted. To add even more space for tourists, the Whispering Pines Motel was built next to the Aztec Hotel in 1956.

Sadly, the Aztec was destroyed by fire in 1958, after the Illgens retired. As for the little cabinolas, they were sold off in the late 1960s to make way for what is today Highway 61. Just a few remain intact, in the hands of private owners. Incidentally, Rudy Illgen had a patent not only on the cabinolas but on several other inventions as well, including the "United States Aero Dreadnaught and Auto-Plane"—the forerunner to the helicopter.

When Rudy wasn't busy creating some new invention or dreaming up ways to make money, he wrote a book called *Silver Avenue*. Rudy envisioned the North Shore as one long street, the longest in the world. Some would argue that the increasing development pressure along Highway 61 shows he wasn't far off in his prophecy.

All that remains of Rudy Illgen's empire is the Whispering Pines Motel. There isn't much else, except a simple green and white highway sign that marks the site of what had been Illgen City: "Pop. 4. Room for Lots More."

3M AND CRYSTAL BAY

One of Minnesota's largest and best-known firms had an inauspicious start on the North Shore. What remains of this endeavor is along Highway 61, far down a steep embankment, on the shores of Lake Superior.

At the turn of the twentieth century, much of the talk in northeastern Minnesota centered on mining. Whether it was iron ore around Lake Vermilion or copper found near the French River, searching for precious metals was the focus of many men hoping to strike it rich.

A Duluth prospector named Ed Lewis was one such dreamer. He reportedly discovered a rich cache of corundum—a natural abrasive whose hardness is second only to diamonds—around the Baptism River. Lewis and others formed the Minnesota Abrasive Company, which ran out of money before any mineral was even dug out of the ground. However, an interest in corundum and an eye for profitable ventures spurred another group of men into action. In 1902, a physician, a butcher, two railroad men, and a lawyer met in Two Harbors and formed the Minnesota Mining and Manufacturing Company, eventually known as 3M.

The original corundum crushing plant on Lake Superior, ca. 1910

The men moved quickly. A site was selected for a corundum crushing plant on Crystal Bay, a lovely spot with a graceful sweep of shoreline and a unique sea cave carved out of the rocky cliff that shelters part of the bay. A large dock, a six-story crushing mill, and a warehouse were built, along with an aerial tramway reaching about a half mile back into the woods, where the corundum mine was.

As with any new venture, there were high hopes for the Minnesota Mining and Manufacturing Company of Two Harbors. The firm set up an office and warehouse in Chicago and in March 1904 sold one ton of corundum to the Champion Corundum Wheel Company of that city. It was Minnesota Mining and Manufacturing's first and last corundum sale.

The mineral mined near Crystal Bay wasn't corundum at all. Rather, it was anorthosite, a worthless rock, too soft to do anything with. One thing led to another, and in the fall of 1904 the stock of the 3M Company was practically as worthless as the anorthosite it was mining. The firm sought a "higher grade" of corundum and sent an expedition to Carlton Peak near Tofte in March 1907. Copper, not corundum, was found there.

In an attempt to save 3M, the founders decided to make sandpaper. Two wealthy St. Paul businessmen agreed not only to buy a controlling interest in the struggling company but to lend it money to get the sandpaper business up and running in Duluth. There they hit another snag: the climate along the waterfront was too damp, and the sandpaper wouldn't dry well. One of the investors, Lucius P. Ordway, who had sunk about two hundred thousand dollars into the company and wanted to keep an eye on his investment, demanded that the operations be moved to St. Paul. The

ONE OF THE MOST BEAUTIFUL SITES ON THE NORTH SHORE IS LOCATED A FEW MILES NORTH OF SILVER BAY. PALISADE HEAD IS A SHEER VERTICAL WALL OF ROCK 314 FEET ABOVE LAKE LEVEL. ON A CLEAR DAY, THE APOSTLE ISLANDS MAY BE SEEN SOME THIRTY MILES OFFSHORE.

Footings of the original corundum plant

sandpaper plant was relocated in 1910, but the corporate offices remained in Two Harbors.

The Crystal Bay mine and crushing plant were shut down and sold in 1916. All ties to Two Harbors were cut as well. However, Ordway and others started to see their investment take off. The firm grew from making sandpaper to creating a transparent cellophane tape—Scotch Tape— that became one of the most recognizable trademarks in the world. Over the decades, 3M employees have created any number of well-known products, and the firm stands as one of Minnesota's largest and most successful.

What remains of 3M's Crystal Bay roots is now part of Tettegouche State Park. The mill's cement footings are covered with moss. Old bricks are strewn on the forest floor. Much of the site has been buried under tons of fill for Highway 61. But a careful look on the uphill side of the highway reveals part of a tramway tower that used to carry "corundum" to the Lake Superior shoreline— along with the hopes of those tenacious entrepreneurs from Two Harbors.

MATTSON FISH HOUSE

The Edward and Lisa Mattson home in East Beaver Bay, built in 1902 and listed in the National Register of Historic Places in 1990

If today's travelers could go back to Highway 61 in the 1920s, '30s, and '40s—when it was Highway 1—they would be surprised to see the number of fishing shacks and boathouses along the North Shore. Wide fishnets stretched out on racks to dry and a buzz of activity surrounded most boat launches. Very few reminders of this era remain. One of the best preserved is the Edward and Lisa Mattson home and their fish house next door. The Mattson place is at the bottom of a steep hill outside East Beaver Bay, steps away from a quiet Lake Superior cove.

The charming whitewashed log cottage and weathered fish house represent the kind of small, family-owned commercial fishing operations that were common along the shore in the late nineteenth and early twentieth centuries. In the 1840s, before Minnesota was even a state, Lake Superior's "inexhaustible" abundance of fish was touted in various publications. Lawmakers eyed the potential economic benefits of Lake Superior as a commercial fishery, and land speculators used the information as fodder to entice new settlers to the region.

Edward Mattson, an immigrant from Norway, and his wife, Lisa, were among the new faces who made their way up the shore. They moved from Duluth to the Beaver Bay area in 1907. Edward originally thought he'd hire on as a fisherman, but he wound up buying a boat and fishing the waters of Lake Superior on his own. The Mattsons joined other families like the Toftes, Crofts, Fenstads, Sves, and Jacobsens, all of them tending nets and trying to make a living off their small commercial fishing operations. Many of these new immigrants were from fishing families in their former countries: heading out on chilly Lake Superior in a tiny wooden skiff was almost second nature.

By 1917, there were 273 licensed commercial fishermen along the shore. The number continued to grow, as did the catches of fish pulled from the lake. By 1936, more than four hundred licensed commercial fishermen worked along the North Shore. Annual catches in the 1930s and '40s averaged between four and eight million pounds of lake trout, whitefish, and herring.

Pulling in all that fish was tough work. Tough and dangerous: some men never made it back to shore when storms blew in. The fishermen got up before dawn every morning, launched their small skiffs, and checked their nets. A gentleman's agreement kept them from fishing their neighbor's territory. Gill nets were set about two to five miles out and one to two miles across from a fisherman's house. Some say there were so many nets in the lake between Knife River and Duluth that they could stretch from the Atlantic to the Pacific—and some of today's fisheries experts can almost believe it.

Gertrude and Alphonse Anderson of Palmers preparing smoked ciscoes for packaging, ca. 1940s

Gill netting is a pretty simple process. The fish swim into the nets, and while their heads can get through the mesh, their bodies can't. The more they wiggle, the more trapped they become, tangled by their gills. But pulling up nets full of thrashing fish was not easy. Alvin Anderson would go out with his father, Alphonse, and "pick" the nets. The Andersons lived on Bonus Point, close to the Sucker River.

Anderson's father didn't believe in using rubber gloves to pick fish: he made Alvin use canvas gloves. When they got soggy and stiff in the cold, the gloves were dunked in water, wrung out, and put back on. Clean, dry gloves were allowed on the trip back home.

In the industry's heyday, so many fish were pulled into the small skiffs that fishermen stood up to their knees in the day's catch as they motored or rowed to shore. Cleaning all that fish, along with mending nets and repairing buoys, took up the rest of the day. The wives also had tough duty. Gert Anderson, Alphonse's wife, remembered watching for his boat out on the lake as he set his nets. She would start breakfast, only to put that on hold and rush down to the beach, where she'd winch up the skiff and pull it into the fish house, then turn around and finish preparing the meal before Alphonse got back in the house. The Andersons and other fishing families packed the day's catch into boxes that they hauled out to the road to be picked up by delivery trucks making daily runs into Duluth.

Lake trout was the moneymaker, fetching thirty to forty cents per pound. Some families earned as much as nine thousand dollars a year, a tidy sum in the early 1940s, and if a family needed more money, they'd just put out another net. Many fishing families also sold fresh and smoked fish directly to the tourists who began making their way up Highway 61 in droves. Alphonse and Gert Anderson ran the Anderson Fish Stand near resorts with names like Shorecrest, Lakeview Castle, and Wonderland, not too far out of Duluth.

The phrase "all good things must come to an end" sadly became true for the North Shore's commercial fishermen. The industry was hit by an unhappy set of circumstances in the 1950s and '60s. The exotic, invasive sea lamprey made its way into Lake Superior and hit the lake trout population hard. After pulling in millions of pounds of trout over the years, in 1962 fishermen caught only six hundred pounds and commercial fishing of trout was prohibited. Pollution also hurt fish populations, as did decades of overfishing—or record harvests, depending on your point of view. The decline was so steep and fast that after generations of roaring success many fishermen found themselves pulling in their nets for the last time.

There are now only a handful of commercial fishermen on Lake Superior. One of them is a descendent of Ed Mattson's,

Remnant of the North Shore commercial fishing industry: a boathouse on Chicago Bay in Hovland

and the old fish house is still used for its intended purpose. The Mattson home, considered one of the oldest on the North Shore, remains almost exactly as it did when it was built more than a century ago. Relatives still use the tiny cottage because it is part of their heritage and their roots along the rocky shoreline remain strong. The same can be said of many other families who have called the North Shore home.

SPLIT ROCK LIGHTHOUSE LENS

Thirty-two steps up a steep, narrow spiral staircase lead to the window-filled room that houses the Split Rock Lighthouse beacon. Making their way up and down several times each day, lighthouse keepers had intimate knowledge of every step. Today's visitors are welcome to make that climb, and as many as one hundred thousand do so every year.

Split Rock Lighthouse is a landmark, one of the best-known sites along the North Shore, if not in the entire state. Most people have seen iconic photographs of the lighthouse as it majestically sits above Lake Superior on a rugged, rocky cliff.

The lighthouse was built in 1910 in response to growing concern for mariners as they navigated what could be an unforgiving and inhospitable Lake Superior. In 1905, one storm alone damaged or destroyed twenty-nine ships, many from the U.S. Steel fleet. Company officials demanded quick congressional action. Several years and seventy-five thousand dollars later, the beacon of Split Rock Lighthouse could be seen by vessels twenty-two miles offshore. (Some commercial fishermen swear they could see the glow of the lighthouse beam off the shore of Grand Marais, some sixty miles away.)

Light keepers climbed these stairs at least twice a day to tend to the beacon.

At ten thousand dollars, one of the largest expenditures for the lighthouse was the lens and its assembly. The Parisian-made lens is a third-order bivalve Fresnel that looks like a glittering clamshell when the sun hits it. (There are six sizes, or orders, of lenses. A first-order lens is the most powerful and usually stationed on a seacoast. A sixth-order lens would be a light seen on the end of a pier or breakwater.) The Split Rock lens is seven feet across, and its sparkling prisms are made of soda-lime glass, giving them a slightly greenish tint. Soda-lime glass is more forgiving of temperature extremes than other types of glass.

Despite weighing more than two tons, the lens assembly can be moved by a mere push of a finger because the apparatus sits on a platform floating on a thin bed of liquid mercury. The lens's rotation is provided by a clockwork mechanism driven by gears connected by a series of cables and weights that drop, by gravity, through a hollow mast in the center of the lighthouse tower. As the weights drop, the lens rotates, once every twenty seconds. For mariners miles out to sea, a ten-second flash was their guide, and if they saw such a light on the horizon, they knew they were in the vicinity of Split Rock Lighthouse. Each lighthouse has a distinctive signature of light.

Efforts are under way to raise money to restore the delicate prisms of the lens.

The beacon at Split Rock was initially powered by a kerosene flame that created a brilliant bright light—so powerful that the keepers knew never to look into the beam when the lens was rotating. According to Lee Radzak, longtime manager of the Split Rock Lighthouse historic site, keepers fired up the beacon a half hour before sunset and kept it lit and revolving until a half hour after sunrise every day of the shipping season, mid-April through mid-December. Each night, a two-gallon supply of kerosene was carefully measured out and brought from the oil storage house to the lighthouse, where it was hand pumped into a brass tank. While the weight and cable mechanism that made the lens rotate had to be wound every two hours, the kerosene tank usually kept burning until daybreak. There was, however, one sleepless night in 1926 when the mercury ran low and two keepers had to turn the beacon by hand until the sun came up. When electricity arrived on the North Shore in 1939, the lighthouse beacon was modernized and powered by a thousand-watt lightbulb, easing the lighthouse keepers' responsibilities a bit.

When it came to tidying up the lighthouse, early keepers had specific instructions courtesy their employer, the U.S. Lighthouse Service. Maintaining the light was, of course, the keepers' main job. Once a day, they feather dusted the delicate Fresnel lens prisms; once a week, a little vinegar was used to carefully wipe clean the glass. Streaks were not allowed. The clockworks were inspected, carefully dusted, and oiled every so often.

The U.S. Coast Guard took over Split Rock in 1939, and the lighthouse was decommissioned in 1969. The landmark became property of the state in 1971. The lighthouse has been restored to its pre-1924 glory, a time before highways and tourists, when all that stood between a fierce storm on the lake and the safety of a harbor was the beacon of Split Rock Lighthouse.

SPLIT ROCK RIVER PILINGS

It doesn't take much imagination to see that the two parallel rows of neatly spaced wooden stumps jutting out from the water near the mouth of the Split Rock River were probably a dock of some kind. Mother Nature didn't place them there. Crews from the Split Rock Lumber Company did as part of their logging camp that operated here from 1899 to 1907.

While the Schroeder Lumber Company floated their logs down the Cross River into Lake Superior, the Split Rock Lumber Company brought cut logs out of the woods via a segment of the Split Rock and Northern Railroad, which ran trains to the mouth of the Split Rock River. Those wooden pilings visible today were the footings for a wharf and train trestle. The wharf/trestle was about 184 feet long and about sixteen feet wide—large enough to allow steamers and some lake freighters to land at the lumber company camp.

The logging camp and its operations near the Split Rock River were in full swing in 1903. About 350 men were in the woods cutting trees. Several employees' families lived in the camp near Lake Superior, which had its own store and post office, a warehouse, several shanties, and a coal dock.

Remnants of the Split Rock Lumber Company's operations

According to state archaeologists, the logging trains probably dumped their loads off the trestle and into a dammed-off area, and a sluice was used to run the logs into Lake Superior. At the time, lumber firms floated thousands of logs to their ultimate destinations using log rafts. The rafts were made up of other, larger logs chained together in a teardrop shape; the logs, many headed to sawmills in Duluth, were herded into the middle of the raft, which was towed by a tugboat. The Split Rock Lumber Company's tug was a powerful vessel called the *Gladiator*. Rafting logs on the lake wasn't easy. Lake Superior is mercurial, and the winds and waves can shift on a dime. High winds and rough seas could tear the rafts apart, scattering the logs to wash ashore.

It didn't take long for the Split Rock River's timber resources to be exhausted. The estimated annual shipment of logs from the area was 50 million feet, worth about six hundred thousand dollars. The logging company dismantled its operations around 1907, leaving behind some visual reminders of its work, including the old wooden footings.

SPLIT ROCK TRADING POST

"The absence of kitsch makes life unbearable," wrote Friedensreich Hundertwasser. Mr. Hundertwasser, a free-spirited Austrian artist, may never have had the pleasure of experiencing American roadside kitsch. He certainly would have enjoyed a little piece of it along the North Shore's Highway 61.

Shoehorned between the lake and the highway, with the magnificent Split Rock Lighthouse visible in the distance, was the Split Rock Trading Post. It was not affiliated with the lighthouse, but for a dime tourists could climb a wooden tower and peer into a telescope for a bird's-eye view of the landmark— a memorable experience for impressionable young visitors. At the foot of the stairs was a sign: "Bell rings if you don't pay." The store clerks, who'd notice the occasional errant tourist sneaking up the stairs without dropping a dime in the pay box, had fun tolling a bell that called attention to the sheepish scofflaw. The Split Rock Trading Post wasn't the only kitschy tourist trap in the area: a small souvenir shop located within a few feet of the lighthouse boundaries was manned in

The Split Rock Trading Post (ca. 1960) was in business until it was destroyed by fire in 1999.

the early 1940s by some of the light keepers' children. That privately owned shop closed before the Split Rock Trading Post opened, a bit farther down the highway, in 1960.

The trading post had one goal: entice tourists off the road, out of their cars, and into a store crammed with trinkets and souvenirs. The rubber "Indian" tom-toms, polished agate key chains, and birch-bark bric-a-brac were big sellers. Moccasins were popular, as were the rows of postcards. Another major attrac-

The old lookout tower, formerly a viewing station for Split Rock Lighthouse

tion was the "live caged bears," who were more than happy to eat marshmallows while Mom took a picture. A nearby pile of rocks, hauled up from the beach below, bore a sign: "Free Agates! You Pick 'Em!" The Split Rock Trading Post had a little something for everyone, including a bit of nautical history. A huge boat anchor, in its own special display area, was said to be from the wreck of the *Madeira*, which sank in Lake Superior during the fierce storm of 1905, when dozens of ships were lost or damaged.

The building that once housed the trading post burned in 1999. The rusting boat anchor remains tucked in its weathered kiosk, and the old wooden watch-tower is posted with "No Trespassing" signs. Weeds push up out of the pavement where cars by the dozens used to park.

Places like the Split Rock Trading Post, with its roadside zoo and cheesy knick-knacks, once dotted highways across the country. As times and tastes have changed, the concept of roadside kitsch has become highway history, to the vast regret of those who thought such sites—and sights—made the drive worthwhile.

GOOSEBERRY FALLS STATE PARK REFECTORY

While Split Rock Lighthouse was a big draw along the fledgling International Highway in the mid- to late 1920s, another major attraction would captivate travelers by the middle of the next decade. Six hundred and forty acres of wilderness, including the Gooseberry River and its majestic falls, became the first state park along the North Shore, but it took thousands of hours of backbreaking work by a small army of young men to create it.

The deal was sealed in 1934 when the state of Minnesota bought the land from the estate of a former U.S. senator from Wisconsin, William Vilas. But the park

needed to be cleaned up before any tourists could enjoy its beauty. Decades of logging had left the area littered with downed trees and stumps and deeply rutted roads. The "boys" of the Civilian Conservation Corps were given the assignment of creating amenities at what would become Gooseberry Falls State Park.

The Civilian Conservation Corps or CCC was a government-sponsored program of the Depression era, designed to put young men to work on outdoors projects like planting trees, building roads and park buildings, and fighting forest fires. The mostly eighteen- to nineteen-year-olds lived military style in wilderness camps with barracks and a mess hall, latrines, an infirmary, and officers' quarters. The young men made a dollar a day (about thirty dollars a month) and certainly earned their pay. The physical work, in all kinds of weather, would have worn down just about anyone, but the CCC had a motto: "We Can Take It." And most enrollees did: more than eighty-six thousand Minnesota men served in the CCC over its ten-year run.

CCC "boys" pose before a flagpole at Gooseberry Falls, 1930s.

The Bridgehead Refectory also was the park's visitors center until the 1990s.

At Gooseberry Falls, work crews cleared brush and created roads and built the new park stone by stone. Gooseberry Falls State Park has some of the best examples of rustic style architecture built by CCCers. The rustic style uses native stone and logs to create buildings that blend into the environment. Stunning examples in the

park include the old Bridgehead Refectory off Highway 61, close to the bridge that spans the falls. The refectory cost $4,386 and about fifty-three hundred man-hours, and Bert Keller of Two Harbors remembers each stone. Keller was among several CCCers who learned the art of stone masonry while at Gooseberry. Two Italian-born masons supervised all the stonework in the park. Keller, who was nineteen at the time, said his job was to cut stones, carefully chiseling the rough edges to make them fit into the building's intricate pattern. The masons worked with combinations of red, blue, brown, and black granite, all quarried from Duluth or Beaver Bay.

Gooseberry was officially designated a state park in 1937 and enjoyed instant popularity. As more motorists took to the highway, Gooseberry Falls became a major destination. In fact, newspapers reported that on Sundays the bridge would often be "lined from one end to the other" with curious tourists eager for a glimpse of the rushing falls. The Bridgehead Refectory didn't open until 1939, the last structure completed by the CCC in the park. It was a refreshment stand and served as the park visitors center until 1994.

Most of the CCC "boys" are gone, but their work will always be reflected in the beauty and breathtaking craftsmanship of the Bridgehead Refectory and other CCC-era buildings at Gooseberry Falls State Park.

TWO HARBORS LIGHTHOUSE

The North Shore coastline is guarded by two lighthouses. The most famous is Split Rock; the other is just a few miles away, in Two Harbors. The handsome red brick lighthouse keeps watch over Agate and Burlington bays and the iron ore docks where freighters glide in to be loaded with taconite pellets. (Watching one of the ore boats maneuver in to and out of the docks is a real treat.) The Two Harbors Lighthouse is older than its more famous cousin at Split Rock. Its beacon was lit on April 15, 1892—apparently without fanfare. Regardless, it yielded the brightest nighttime light seen along the North Shore coastline for the next fifteen years.

As more people started using lightbulbs, there was some worry that mariners would confuse the lighthouse's fixed white light with some homeowner's electric lamps. To alleviate this concern, in 1907 a rotating red light was installed, the red provided by crimson-colored screens placed in front of the lens. But access was a problem early on. The light keeper or his assistant had to walk through the private family quarters to reach the tower to tend the beacon. The clockwork-like mechanism had to be cranked up every four hours, day and night. Imagine the keeper creeping through the lighthouse after midnight, with cleaning supplies and oilcans in tow, trying not to disrupt sleeping family members.

The Two Harbors Lighthouse, like the one at Split Rock, had a foghorn, and a darned loud one at that. In *The Light on Agate Bay: The Story of the Two Harbors Lighthouse and Its Keepers,* Dale Congdon gives a convincing example of just how earsplitting the sound was. Fran Carpenter, the young daughter of one of the lighthouse keepers, was on her tricycle one day while her father gave a tour of the lighthouse and its grounds to a group of VIPs. They wanted to hear the foghorn, and

ON THE LAKE SIDE OF HIGHWAY 61 BETWEEN TWO HARBORS AND CASTLE DANGER ARE SEVERAL SETS OF LARGE LOG GATES. THEY BELONG TO THE ENCAMPMENT FOREST ASSOCIATION (EFA), AN ENCLAVE OF HOMES ESTABLISHED BY A GROUP OF WEALTHY TWIN CITIES RESIDENTS IN 1921. THE AREA WAS A SUMMER RETREAT FOR SUCH FAMILIES AS THE PILLSBURYS AND THE DAYTONS.

The Two Harbors Lighthouse is now a bed and breakfast.

dear old Dad obliged. Unfortunately, little Fran was on the walkway between the lighthouse and the fog signal building: the blast of sound was so loud that it shook the poor child off her trike. She wasn't hurt, but she said she never went onto that walkway again. The air compressor that created those bellowing blasts is now ensconced in the Smithsonian Institution in Washington, DC.

The Coast Guard automated the light in 1981, and the last Coast Guard–employed light keeper left the Two Harbors facility in 1987. In 1998, the Coast Guard installed a strobe light, which is what mariners and visitors see today. The lighthouse is now a bed and breakfast, owned and operated by the Lake County Historical Society. Some visitors think the place may be haunted: strange voices and footsteps have been heard at night, and there's even a log for guests to record their supernatural encounters. There is no way of explaining the otherworldly antics. According to *The Light on Agate Bay,* only one person has died in the lighthouse. Theresa Lederle, a daughter of keeper Charles Lederle, was twenty-four when she died of an acute illness there in 1902. Kathy Meyer, wife of the last keeper to tend the Two Harbors light, didn't die in the lighthouse, but her ashes were scattered over Lake Superior just in front of the red brick building in 1999 because she so loved the beautiful surroundings. The reports of shadowy shenanigans are certainly intriguing, and the possibility of "meeting" one of the long-gone spirits adds to the adventure and romance of staying in a historic lighthouse.

TWO HARBORS WAS HOME TO SEVERAL CIGAR FACTORIES IN THE EARLY 1900S. ONE FACTORY EMPLOYED FIVE WORKERS AND CRANKED OUT SOME THIRTY THOUSAND CIGARS A MONTH. THE FIVE-CENT CIGARS WERE MADE OF LOCALLY GROWN TOBACCO. ONE OF THE BEST SELLERS? THE "BELLE OF TWO HARBORS," WHICH WENT FOR TEN CENTS.

Two Harbors High School used to be quite a sight from its perch on a hill overlooking the north side of town, just a few blocks off Highway 61. The building, made of limestone and granite, was a striking cream color with sleek Art Deco styling. Crews of laborers from the Public Works Administration or PWA built it in 1939.

The PWA was part of an alphabet soup of federal agencies designed by Franklin D. Roosevelt's administration to put unemployed people back to work during the Great Depression. The situation was dismal across the country. In 1933, the unemployment rate in Minnesota was estimated at 29 percent. Some areas of the state were even worse: on the Iron Range, joblessness was said to be as high as 70 percent.

Two Harbors High School, ca. 1935

The high school auditorium, with WPA-sponsored murals on either side of the stage, ca. 1940

The federally sponsored Works Progress Administration, which included the PWA, offered hope to struggling families and yielded some impressive accomplishments. Nationally, people were put to work on a number of assignments that ranged from public infrastructure building projects to various kinds of conservation work to creating music, art, books,

43

Detail of the original WPA mural before it was removed from the school

and plays to producing clothing for families on welfare rolls. According to a 1940 report, in Minnesota alone WPA workers had completed 19,510 miles of new road (including parts of Highway 61), built 447 bridges, and completed 1,007 public buildings, including 85 schools. One of them was the Two Harbors High School.

The cost of the school was $585,000, much more than originally planned, but it was quite a building, with a large gymnasium and an auditorium that the *Two Harbors Chronicle* gushed over in an article from February 12, 1940: "The auditorium has glass brick windows with velvet curtains that may be drawn so that movies may be shown in the daytime. The stage curtains are in maroon and gold, making a beautiful stage effect. Overhead lights are neon in a soft red and seats are a mohair back and leather cushions."

The auditorium also boasted two large murals, one on either side of the stage. At the time of the school's open house in February 1940, the murals were not yet complete, but the newspaper reported confidently that when finished they would "be a great piece of artistry." The murals—as well as other fine artworks around the state—were painted by artists employed by the WPA's Federal Art Project. One of the Two Harbors High School murals depicted the story of iron ore from its discovery on the Iron Range to its transportation via rail and steamer. The other included wild-life, farming, fishing, and lumbering scenes and a nod to the region's native people.

The murals—and in fact the school itself—are gone now. The paintings were removed in chunks from the auditoriums' walls, but it's unclear whether they will ever be on public display again. The school was placed on the 2007 list of the Ten Most Endangered Historic Places in Minnesota, compiled by the state's Preservation Alliance. That designation did not stay the wrecking ball, however: the school was demolished in the spring of 2008.

KENDALL'S SMOKE HOUSE

Who would have guessed that a delivery truck breakdown would lead to the creation of one of the North Shore's best-known places to buy smoked fish? It happened one day in the mid-1920s, as W. T. (William Thomas) Kendall was making his usual stops along the shore to pick up the day's catch from area fishermen. On the way to Duluth to deliver the load, the old truck broke down. According to Kendall family lore, a quick-thinking W. T., worried the fish might spoil, decided to sell them to passersby, right off the truck. The gambit worked— so well in fact that W. T. started selling fish out of his little grocery store in Knife River.

That store grew in the 1930s, when W. T. and son Russ added a tavern and dance hall, with live bands, food, slot machines, and beer that was "always five cents." Kendall's quickly became one of the most popular nightspots on the North Shore.

Today the little town of Knife River is much quieter, and so is Russ Kendall's Smokehouse. The old wooden bar is still there, as is an ancient arcade game tucked into a corner, the few remnants of Kendall's rollicking past. Smoked fish continues to be Kendall's signature item. Four generations of the family have smoked slabs of salmon and trout, whole ciscoes and herring—as many as a thousand pounds every day. It is a success story with an unusual lesson: sometimes it pays to have engine trouble.

Russ Kendall's, ca. 1930s

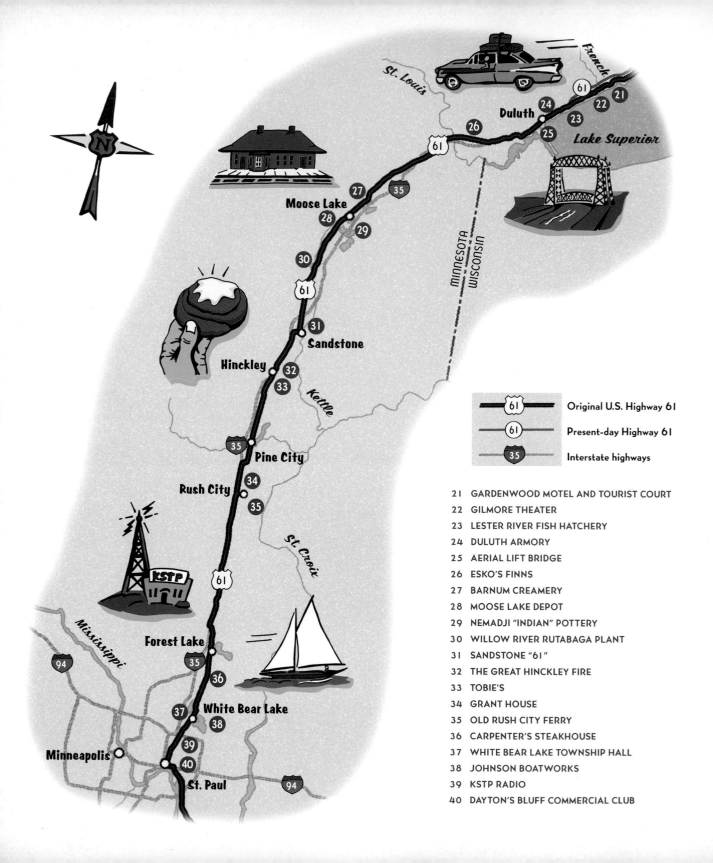

St. Louis

French

Duluth

24

61

22

21

26

23

Lake Superior

25

61

61

27

35

Moose Lake

28

29

30

61

MINNESOTA

WISCONSIN

31

Sandstone

Hinckley

32

33

Kettle

35

Pine City

St. Croix

34

Rush City

35

KSTP

61

Forest Lake

35

Mississippi

36

94

37

White Bear Lake

38

Minneapolis

39

40

St. Paul

94

61 **Original U.S. Highway 61**

61 **Present-day Highway 61**

35 **Interstate highways**

21   GARDENWOOD MOTEL AND TOURIST COURT

22   GILMORE THEATER

23   LESTER RIVER FISH HATCHERY

24   DULUTH ARMORY

25   AERIAL LIFT BRIDGE

26   ESKO'S FINNS

27   BARNUM CREAMERY

28   MOOSE LAKE DEPOT

29   NEMADJI "INDIAN" POTTERY

30   WILLOW RIVER RUTABAGA PLANT

31   SANDSTONE "61"

32   THE GREAT HINCKLEY FIRE

33   TOBIE'S

34   GRANT HOUSE

35   OLD RUSH CITY FERRY

36   CARPENTER'S STEAKHOUSE

37   WHITE BEAR LAKE TOWNSHIP HALL

38   JOHNSON BOATWORKS

39   KSTP RADIO

40   DAYTON'S BLUFF COMMERCIAL CLUB

THE GARDENWOOD TOURIST CABINS

ONLY.

PLACE
STAMP
HERE

Duluth to
St. Paul

61 In the early days of motor touring, intrepid travelers would often sleep in their cars or pitch tents alongside the route. Starting in the mid-1920s, the choices for tired tourists increased with modern campgrounds that had running water and restrooms. If the traveler wasn't interested in sleeping on the ground in a tent, "cabin camps" or "tourist courts" offered the option of parking right next to a tiny cabin. Some of the "ultra modern" cabins had indoor biffies. Some did not. What they all offered was a little more comfort and privacy than sleeping under the stars.

One vestige of those early tourist courts is the Gardenwood Motel and Cabin Court, located a few miles north of Duluth on "scenic" 61, the original highway that fronts the shore. Built by Victor Elmgren in 1929, it originally was known as Elmgren's Tourist Court and offered "20 clean, completely modern cabins" at "moder-

The Gardenwood, originally known as Elmgren's, 1930s

ate rates." The promotional material called it a "hayfever haven," and Elmgren's grandson Dudley recalls that people suffering from allergies would come in such numbers that there was hardly a place to stay between Duluth and the Canadian border.

With slot machines in the back room and a gas pump out front, the family found a number of ways to make money. They offered a few groceries, and Grandma Elmgren fried up trout dinners and sold them for a buck.

The Elmgrens sold the place in 1955. Amazingly enough, today's Gardenwood Motel and Tourist Court has remained virtually the same after all these years, except for repairs and some remodeling. Even a couple of ghosts seem to have stuck around. The current owners say some guests have seen two men wearing robes, smoking cigars, and looking as if they've just come out of the old sauna. On second glance, the men vanish. Places like the Gardenwood have also vanished over the years to make way for larger, more modern motels, vacation condos, and townhouses or other development. With luck, the Gardenwood Motel and Tourist Court will remain a piece of highway history that can be enjoyed by future generations—ghosts included.

The Gardenwood tourist cabins

GILMORE THEATER

61

Two of the thousands of hay fever sufferers who trekked to the North Shore for relief each summer were a certain dashing gentleman and his lovely daughter. If the man looked somewhat familiar, there was good reason: Paul Gilmore was a silent film star, Broadway actor, and theater producer. He would finish his career on Minnesota's North Shore, just steps off of Highway 61.

Paul Gilmore's life could have been fodder for one of his melodramas. According to the biography patrons of the Gilmore Theater received with their playbill, Gilmore had a role in the first moving picture ever made in the United States. Sixty seconds long and filmed on the roof of the American Biograph Company in New York in the 1890s, *The Pillow Fight* starred Gilmore and eight child actors in nighties. The Biograph Company, with director D. W. Griffith at the helm, eventually boasted a stable of stars that included Mary Pickford and Lionel Barrymore. Gilmore performed in a number of silent films between 1900 and 1910 and additionally spent a fair amount of time on the stage. While he did play Broadway, Gilmore also spent months traveling cross-country with stage productions—a schedule that seems to have caused problems in his personal life. According to the *New York Times* of January 2, 1909, Mrs. Mary Alice Goodwin Gilmore was granted a divorce on the grounds of "desertion and non support." Mr. Gilmore married someone else a few months later.

Aerial view of Gilmore Theater, ca. 1950

Paul Gilmore and daughter Virginia, souvenir program

The handsome actor/producer/director was apparently also a dreamer. Gilmore thought Florida's Manatee County area could one day rival Hollywood for filmmaking. According to the *Manatee River Journal* of December 1, 1921, Gilmore bought forty acres at the south end of Coquina Beach, planning to transform it into Paul Gilmore's Oriental Film City, complete with a subdivision of beach cottages, a bathhouse, a boathouse, and a waterslide. The subdivision was renamed Gil-Mor Isle. Glimmers of his dream came true when the Character Picture Corporation wanted to shoot *The Isle of Destiny* on Gil-Mor Isle. Gilmore starred as a wealthy plantation owner shipwrecked on a desert island with his lady love: fire destroys his ship, savages attack, and our hero rescues (and gets) the girl. The movie was never distributed nationally. Similar attempts at moviemaking fell flat, as did Gilmore's dream of building a film colony in Florida.

Sometime in the thirties, Paul Gilmore felt "compelled to return to his chosen profession" and began acting on the stage, even taking over the Cherry Lane Theater, one of New York's oldest, and staging a new play every two weeks for three years.

It isn't clear just when Gilmore discovered the North Shore. He and his daughter Virginia first came to Duluth with relatives from Iowa as they sought relief from hay fever. They returned summer after summer, and in 1944 the aging actor announced he was going to build a theater that would be "modern architecture personified" on one hundred feet of lake frontage just east of the French River. The "modern architecture" was a large, silver Quonset hut that could seat two hundred and was "fire proof, sun proof and bomb proof" but looked a bit out of place along woodsy Lake Superior.

The Gilmore Comedy Theater took as its motto "A Theater for all the People," as the Gilmores staged "Broadway hits at popular prices." Virginia starred in most of her father's productions, including the theater's opening performance of *This Thing Called Love* in July 1949. The summer theater was taken over in 1957 by three Twin Cities men, including the legendary Don Stolz of the Old Log Theater in Excelsior, who ran it for one summer on Gilmore's request, calling it Theater 61.

Stolz remembers the Gilmores as "delightful people" and Paul as a legitimate actor who made an attempt at serious theater on the shores of Lake Superior. Margaret Morris, the grand dame reporter of Twin Cities society pages, agreed, writing in the Minneapolis newspaper that the Gilmore Theater was "the first venture in straw-hat playmaking attempted in this vicinity."

All plays have a final act, and the Gilmore Theater's came in the late 1950s. The structure was unceremoniously torn down, and now only a concrete slab remains by the lake.

LESTER RIVER FISH HATCHERY

61 The trout, herring, and whitefish raised at the Lester River Fish Hatchery in Duluth had some pretty fancy digs. The cream-colored confection of a building still stands by the mouth of the Lester River on London Road, a few blocks from where "scenic" 61 and the expressway converge. The hatchery was built around 1887, and the Victorian influence is obvious. The building's eaves and gables are adorned with carved brackets, and sections of the exterior are covered in scalloped shingles, giving the place a gingerbread-house feel. It's an elegant

U.S. Fish Hatchery at the Lester River showing fish tanks at rear of building, 1910

The fish hatchery is a lovely example of the stick and shingle style popular in the 1880s.

building that had a pretty messy use: nurturing millions of fish.

The Lester River Fish Hatchery was the only federal facility of its kind on Lake Superior. Officials pushed to get it built as commercial fishing on the lake became a major business. The state fish commission's 1886 annual report declared that group's intention to not only improve fishing on Lake Superior but to make Duluth a world leader in fish production. In order to achieve those lofty goals, the hatchery's main work was to stock the lake with whitefish—considered by many to be the most delicious local species—and lake trout.

The Duluth station had the capacity to hatch 150 million fish eggs—more than two similar federal facilities in Michigan combined. Long narrow troughs were installed inside and outside the building to rear tens of thousands of young fish. The effort was bolstered by area fishermen, who brought in fertilized fish eggs each fall. In the spring, milk cans were lugged to the shores of the lake or to the banks of area streams and the tiny fish released.

The state of Minnesota got into the business of raising fish when it opened the French River Hatchery a few miles up the North Shore in 1918. The hatcheries worked together, transferring fish between the two facilities for many years.

At midcentury, the federal government announced plans to close the Lester River Hatchery, citing inefficiencies. Calls to modernize the facility and keep it open came from commercial fishermen and civic leaders, who had become "increasingly alarmed" about heavy fishing pressure on the lake with no propagation program to renew the resource. Their requests fell on deaf governmental ears. Water issues also contributed to the hatchery's downfall: the river temperature at times was too warm, and fish, especially trout, need cold water to survive and thrive. The French River Hatchery, still in operation, has a better source of cold water, which is key to raising fish. The Lester River Fish Hatchery, having outlived its usefulness, was shut down in the fall of 1946.

Seizing an opportunity, the University of Minnesota at Duluth converted the building into a freshwater research facility. Studies throughout the 1960s and '70s, in conjunction with the federal Environmental Protection Agency, gathered information on important dangers—such as acid rain and mercury contamination—

facing Lake Superior and northeastern Minnesota. After those research projects ran their course, the building, expensive to maintain, sat virtually unused.

Stacks of coolers are stored in the building's basement, filled with tubes of lake water and sediment used in past research projects. The outlines of the original fish tanks are still visible on the floor. Now the former Lester River U.S. Fish Hatchery and University of Minnesota–Duluth Limnological Research Facility awaits a new purpose. At present, there are plans to turn it into an interpretive center for visitors going up the North Shore.

DULUTH ARMORY

61 Heading south, Highway 61 enters Duluth on Superior Street, and a building that has a little something to do with the storied highway stands just a block away, fronting London Road. The Duluth Armory is an imposing brick building with an impressive history. *Impressive* also describes the building's size: several stories and more than one hundred thousand square feet.

Built in 1915, just before World War I, the armory served as the training center for Minnesota National Guard and Naval Militia units. The drill room for the troops was nearly as big as a football field so platoons could master marching. Sand was trucked in so the soldiers could practice digging foxholes, too. In 1918, the armory became an emergency shelter, housing victims of the forest fires that devastated Cloquet and Moose Lake.

Besides military and emergency uses, the Duluth Armory played host to a roster of famous entertainers, artists, and politicians. Acts ranging from Johnny Cash to Louis Armstrong to Arthur Fiedler and the Boston Pops headlined the armory. Cowboy movie star Roy Rogers showed up with his trusty horse, Trigger; comedian Bob Hope brought down the house;

The "new" armory, ca. 1915

The Duluth Armory's future is unknown.

and then there was that Buddy Holly concert in January 1959, one of the rock legend's final shows before he died in a plane crash in Iowa. Holly shared the stage with other of the era's big rock and roll bands, including the Big Bopper, Ritchie Valens, and Dion and the Belmonts. In the audience that night, right up front, was young Robert Zimmerman of Hibbing. Zimmerman—better known as Bob Dylan—became something of a musical legend himself.

Born in Duluth, Bob moved with his family to Hibbing when he was six years old. He and an auditorium full of other teens witnessed the concert that night, and Dylan has said that the experience inspired his career. As Dylan accepted the 1997 Grammy Award for Best Album, he said, "when I was about sixteen or seventeen years old, I went to see Buddy Holly play at the Duluth National Guard Armory, and I was three feet away from him and he looked at me and . . . I know he was with us all the time we were making this record in some kind of way." Rare are the comments Dylan has made about his Duluth roots.

Yet one of Dylan's most famous albums is *Highway 61 Revisited*—and thus the highway's connection to the armory is revealed. Many agree the album was a seminal break with Dylan's early folksy style. *Highway 61 Revisited* incorporates electric guitars, and for experts the songs demonstrate that Dylan was finding his own voice, independent from traditional blues- or folk-based music. What about Highway 61 prompted Dylan to write the title track? The road stretches from the tip of northeastern Minnesota to New Orleans and the Mississippi Delta. It has been called the "blues highway," and it appears to have been Dylan's road to the rest of the world. In his 2004 *Chronicles,* Dylan writes a bit about the highway and how he feels a spiritual kinship with it: "Highway 61, the main thoroughfare of the country blues, begins about where I came from . . . Duluth to be exact. I always felt like I'd started on it, always had been on it, and could go anywhere from it, even down into the deep Delta country. It was the same road, full of the same contradictions, the same one-horse towns, the same spiritual ancestors."

In 2007, street signs were posted in Duluth designating sections of certain roads "Bob Dylan Way." One part of this "cultural pathway" runs in front of the Duluth Armory. After decades of concerts, home shows, proms, high school basketball tournaments, professional wrestling matches, and military funerals, the Duluth Armory became a garage for city vehicles in the 1970s. Today it is mostly empty. Paint peels in the ballroom overlooking Lake Superior; the hardwood floor buckles in spots. Now the venerable building—listed as one of Minnesota's Most Endangered Historic Places by the state's Preservation Alliance—awaits a new assignment.

AERIAL LIFT BRIDGE

61 The most recognizable landmark in Duluth would have to be the Aerial Lift Bridge. People flock to the waterfront in almost any weather to watch the oceangoing ships and Great Lakes freighters glide under the bridge and into the harbor—but only after the vessels bellow a rumbling salute to the lift bridge operator.

The need for the bridge became apparent in 1871 after crews dug through the narrow spit of land known as Minnesota Point in order to open up the harbor for shipping. While this engineering feat was considered a great achievement, folks living on Park Point were cut off from the mainland. Ferries were used for a time, and temporary bridges were built during the winter months.

In order to tackle the problem head-on, Duluth's city leaders sponsored a bridge design contest in 1892. They wanted a bridge that would let residents and delivery wagons go back and forth but also allow ships access to the harbor. Most of the proposals involved variations of swing bridges or bascule bridges (which are similar to drawbridges). Those designs met with disapproval from army engineers and ship operators, who thought they'd impede boat traffic. The winning plan came from

The Aerial Ferry Bridge— with gondola—ca. 1920

John Alexander Low Waddell. Had it been built, the span would have been the world's first high-rise vertical lift bridge, but the plans were shelved. Waddell's design called for a big bridge accessible to trains as well as to foot and wagon traffic, and the shipping companies worried that marine traffic would be blocked as trains rumbled over the substantial span. Waddell, none too happy, took his design to Chicago and built what is now known as the South Halsted Street Bridge.

A second attempt was made by city engineer Thomas McGilvray, his design inspired by a bridge in France. It looked a bit like today's bridge, except a huge gondola slid cars and carriages back and forth instead of a deck moving up and down. After a lack of funds in 1902 paused construction, the Duluth Aerial Ferry Bridge was finally completed, opening in 1905. It could carry up to one hundred and twenty-five thousand pounds, which might include a loaded streetcar, 350 passengers, and a couple of horse and wagon teams. The gondola could cross the channel in about one minute, and trips were made a dozen times a day between five in the morning and midnight. Most importantly, any of the Great Lakes vessels could comfortably pass under the bridge and into the harbor.

As Duluth grew, so did traffic levels, and in the late 1920s the gondola was removed and the bridge's height increased to 227 feet. It was modified to include a deck that could move up and down to accommodate outbound and inbound ships but could also handle a flow of vehicle traffic when in the lowered position. The changes, ironically enough, made the bridge much like the original design of 1892. The first vessel to travel under the remodeled Aerial Lift Bridge was the tug *Essaysons* on March 29, 1930. Since then, the bridge lifts to accommodate boat traffic an average of five thousand times a year, close to twenty-five to thirty times a day, taking about three minutes to raise the deck to its full height. All that activity is testament to the bridge's solid design and construction.

The Aerial Lift Bridge is the gateway to the Port of Duluth, which is one of the busiest on the Great Lakes. At one point in the 1900s, Duluth surpassed New York City in the amount of tonnage handled. The port still ships millions of tons of coal, taconite, wheat, and other products. An estimated five hundred thousand tourists visit the harbor each year, and no matter the weather there always seem to be curious onlookers captivated by the sight of the mammoth ships as they slip underneath one of Duluth's most enduring icons.

An oceangoing ship entering the Duluth/Superior Harbor underneath the Aerial Lift Bridge

61 Motorists driving through Esko on what is County Road 61 but also the old Highway 61 will notice a cluster of weathered wooden buildings— evidence of Esko's rich Finnish history. Esko owes its name to Peter Esko, who made his way here in 1873, one of an impressive wave of Finnish immigrants to America. Between 1870 and 1920, an estimated three hundred forty thousand Finns arrived in this country.

TO SOUND LIKE AN AUTHENTIC FINN, PRONOUNCE *SAUNA* AS *SOW*-NUH, NOT *SAW*-NUH.

Minnesota was a popular spot for these newcomers: in fact, so many Finns settled in Duluth that it was called the "Helsinki of America." Esko was nearly 100 percent Finn in its early years. The chilly climate and the forests and bogs had something to do with it, especially for the very first Finnish arrivals. It reminded them of home.

The Finns brought with them certain customs that may have puzzled their new neighbors. The Finnish ritual of sitting in sweltering saunas evidently caught the attention of a wary farmer near Esko. In the *WPA Guide to Minnesota,* published in 1938, the entry for Esko conveys some cultural confusion. A local farmer claimed that every day entire families, wrapped in sheets, would troop into small wooden buildings on their property for the purpose of worshipping pagan gods, petitioning good harvests for Finns and "wrath upon their neighbors."

While it was true the Finns wrapped themselves in sheets, it wasn't to worship in what outsiders thought was a "shrine"; rather, it was to take hot steamy baths—the Finnish version of a shower. Finns do revere their saunas, an attitude reflected in the Finnish saying "in the sauna, you must behave as in a church." For some Finns, it seems, the old American saying "cleanliness is next to Godliness" may hold some water.

Today, an old sauna sits close to a Finnish-made home and barn just off the main drag in Esko, part of a small exhibit on the town's extensive Finnish roots created by the Esko Historical Society.

An old sauna, one of several Finnish buildings on display in downtown Esko

61

Barnum's reputation as the epicenter of northeastern Minnesota agriculture was built on cows and chickens. Not just any chickens, and not some run-of-the-mill cows. The hub of all the activity was a solidly built brick creamery at the edge of town.

The chicken and egg tale spun in the 1938 WPA *Guide to Minnesota* about Barnum's rise as a poultry powerhouse revolves around a lumberjack who returned to his hometown to earn easy money raising chickens. He invested all his savings in a farm and stocked it with two thousand birds. The neighbors, so the story goes, were skeptical the chicks would survive the bitterly cold northland winter, but five hundred made it to spring. The rookie farmer pressed on, and eventually his hard work paid off: Barnum, the book went on to say, became one of Minnesota's largest egg-producing centers.

That last part is true, although it appears the rest of the tale is not. The real story, however, is almost as good.

The man behind the bright idea to raise chickens was H. C. Hanson. When the Hanson family arrived in Barnum in 1903, it found a struggling little burg with a handful of stores and a few rundown homes. The major business in town, the creamery, was floundering and literally falling apart. Hanson founded the State Bank of Barnum and realized that only a vital industry could save the town. In 1907 he called together area farmers and put a proposition on the table: he'd buy the old creamery and find a market for their eggs and milk, but the farmers had to agree to specialize in one type of chicken and one breed of cow. Hanson figured that if egg and milk production were successful, his bank would be, too.

Area farmers made their decision. The chickens of choice were White Leghorns, and the cows that made the cut were Guernseys. Hanson kept his promise to fix up the creamery, and he loaned money so farmers could improve their buildings and get into the poultry and dairy business. The chickens quickly became moneymakers: the creamery paid seventeen cents per dozen eggs, much more than farmers had pre-

THE SWINGING BRIDGE IN JAY COOKE STATE PARK NEAR CARLTON IS ONE OF ONLY TWO SUSPENSION BRIDGES IN ANY OF MINNESOTA'S STATE PARKS. THE RUSTIC STYLE BUILDINGS WERE ALL CONSTRUCTED BY THE CCC BETWEEN 1933 AND 1942.

The Barnum Creamery in its heyday, ca. 1910–20

viously made. As word spread of this success, more farmers wanted a piece of the action. One established a hennery with two thousand chickens—might this be the gentleman of WPA fame?—but most had flocks of fifty to one hundred birds.

By 1912, Barnum eggs were being ordered by fine New York City restaurants, and some poultry farms were growing ever larger to meet demand. In the 1920s, Barnum was second only to Petaluma, California, in breeding White Leghorn chickens, and the Barnum egg

The former Barnum Creamery, now empty

business kept growing—as did the local dairy industry. Living up to its name, the creamery specialized in sweet cream butter. The butter, like the eggs, earned a national reputation. In fact, President Calvin Coolidge, who vacationed in Brule, Wisconsin, reportedly sent his cooks to Duluth to buy Barnum butter. Not wanting to pass up good PR, Hanson put up billboards that read "Chief Executive Eats Barnum Butter."

The difficult economic times of the 1930s affected Barnum's farmers, but the town still gained national and even international attention when twenty-five of their best Guernsey milking cows were shipped to Shanghai, China. Eggs and milk continued as mainstays of the local economy in the 1940s and '50s, but things changed in 1961 when Old Home Creameries sold the Barnum facility to a Superior,

The creamery's products drew accolades.

Wisconsin, co-op and the Barnum creamery closed for good.

The town itself changed dramatically after November 1969, when the northbound lanes of Interstate 35 opened from the Twin Cities to Scanlon. Traffic levels on Highway 61, formerly the main route into Barnum, slowed to a trickle, and so did the revenue from businesses that catered to travelers. One by one, established firms closed or moved closer to busy I-35. Today, downtown Barnum is a quiet place. But one building remains in the same spot as it has since 1895: the Barnum creamery, empty now, built by the dreams of generations of area farmers and a man by the name of H. C. Hanson.

61 Highway 61 is just a few blocks east of what used to be a main route in to and out of Moose Lake: the Soo Line Railroad. Still standing alongside the old railroad bed is a carefully restored depot, painted a cheery pale gold and maroon, looking very much the way it did when it was built for the Minneapolis, St. Paul and Sault Ste. Marie (Soo) Railroad in the 1870s. The depot is one of Moose Lake's most historic buildings—and an appropriate monument to the town's past. Moose Lake began as a stagecoach stop, with a handful of homes and a hotel in the 1860s. Once the railroad came through, the town experienced a growth spurt, with more businesses and residents moving in. The Soo Line depot was built around 1873, providing an important refueling stop for those early trains that burned wood to keep their engines chugging along. Decades later, a spark from one of those trains may have ignited one of Minnesota's worst disasters.

The summer of 1918 had been hot and dry, and the fall brought little rain. A windy day on October 12 combined with tinder-dry conditions and some kind of spark, perhaps from a passing train, to fuel a deadly wildfire. In fact, high winds may have fanned the flames of several fires, merging them into one gigantic wall of flame.

The fires consumed hundreds of acres of land from Sturgeon Lake through Moose Lake, into parts of Carlton County, and on to St. Louis County and Duluth. Cloquet suffered the most damage: most of the town was left in ashes. The fire, pushed by wind gusts of seventy miles per hour, moved so fast that in many cases there was no time to run. People who tried to escape in trucks and cars on Highway

The Soo Line depot, a museum run by the Moose Lake Area Historical Society

73 south of Kettle River drove off the road because of thick smoke, and a chain-reaction pileup killed twenty-five people on what is still called "Dead Man's Curve." Those who weren't fortunate enough to have a means of escape covered themselves with wet blankets and hunkered down in plowed fields. Others hid from the flames in wells or root cellars; they suffocated as the fierce flames sucked away their oxygen. One account tells of a family whose supper was in the oven when they were forced to run for their lives. Upon their return, the house was gone but the cast iron stove was still standing—and their meal was ready to eat. What the fire left behind pales in comparison to the terrible toll it took.

Moose Lake after fire, 1918

In all, 453 people died and fifty-two thousand homes were destroyed, along with thirty-eight communities. Survivors were put up for the winter in "fire shacks" built by Red Cross volunteers. When the cold and snow arrived, so did a second blow: the 1918–19 influenza epidemic, which claimed many lives that the fire had not. Still, the people of Moose Lake decided to rebuild, and today the renovated Soo Line depot houses a museum that tells their stories of heroism and tragedy in the face of the disastrous fires of 1918. The depot is also a popular rest stop for bike, ATV, and snowmobile riders. The iron tracks that used to carry the trains of the Minneapolis, St. Paul and Sault Ste. Marie (Soo) Railroad are gone, replaced by a ribbon of asphalt and gravel that now carries the Soo Line Trail.

NEMADJI "INDIAN" POTTERY

One of the first businesses to rise from the ashes of the 1918 fire was the Northern Clay Products Corporation of Nemadji Township, just north of Moose Lake. The fire of 1918, which roared through nearly forty towns, created a huge demand for fireproof goods, and brick was one of them. But the product the company became best known for was aimed at tourists in the 1920s, '30s, and '40s.

In 1923, the owners of Northern Clay Products realized their little brick-making operation couldn't successfully compete with a larger firm in Wrenshall. They decided to specialize in decorative tiles and pottery and moved to an area along the railroad tracks close to the Moose Lake depot. The firm was renamed the Nemadji Tile and Pottery Company.

They built kilns to fire handmade, earth-toned tiles, using clay hand dug from pits east of Moose Lake. Some of the rich brown, red, tan, and yellow tiles were plain; others were carved with flowers, birds, and animals. Nemadji tile became instantly popular, snapped up by wealthy homeowners for floors and fireplaces. The tiles were installed in dozens of churches across the country and in schools such as the College of St. Catherine in St. Paul. Tiles by the boxcar were sent out, and the kilns roared into overtime to meet demand.

The Nemadji "Indian" pottery plant in Kettle River, now closed; note kiln at left

As the tile business took off, Nemadji expanded into pottery. Nothing fancy: just utilitarian crocks, bowls, and vases, hand thrown on a foot-operated wheel. One of the owners, Clayton James (C. J.) Dodge, thought the company should make pottery molds to mass-produce items for the fast-growing tourist trade. That idea didn't sit well with co-owner Frank Johnson, who soon left the company. Their tiff paved the way for the creation of the cleverly marketed and very popular Nemadji Indian Pottery.

It is hard to miss Nemadji pottery. The vases, bowls, and other vessels are fired to either a creamy or a dark red tint, and they are bathed in a swirl of bright colors that flow throughout the piece.

A lot of tourist pottery was already on the market in the late twenties and early thirties. In order to get his product on the shelves of trading posts and gift shops nationwide, C. J. Dodge had to create some kind of buzz, a story surrounding the origin of Moose Lake pottery. A Native theme seemed appropriate given the region where the clay was found. *Nemadji* is an Ojibwe word that loosely translated means "left hand." The Nemadji River, which flows through the clay beds of northeastern Minnesota, supposedly earned its name because of its location on the left as Natives walked from Lake Superior to the St. Louis River. The bottom of each colorful, eye-catching pot was stamped with a picture of an arrowhead and the words "Nemadji Tile and Pottery Co. Moose Lake, Minn" or simply "Handmade Nemadji Indian Pottery (from Native Clay)."

Capitalizing on the myths Euro-American tourists believed about the "noble red man," Dodge wrote a "history" of Nemadji Pottery in which he said, "Research has shown us how to imitate the pottery made from these same clays by the ancient Ojibwe tribes who for long centuries ruled the Arrowhead County. Nemadji pottery expresses the soul of the Arrowhead Country and of the Redman who, though long since gone to the Happy Hunting Ground, still haunts our shores and woods." A card outlining this "history" was slipped into each Nemadji pot as proof of its authenticity, and reality became confused with myth. Some trinket shops posted signs by their displays that read "Made by the Nemadji Indians of Minnesota." Shopkeepers did little to clear up the misconception. White tourists bought the fantasy and the pottery, and both the merchants and the manufacturer made money.

Distinctive Nemadji pottery

Nemadji Tile and Pottery continued to operate in Moose Lake until 1973, when it was sold and the operations moved to an old creamery in Kettle River. Almost immediately, the new owners decided to quit using native clay because they felt the thick, clammy soil had inconsistent properties. Instead, they bought cheaper white clay from Iowa and Kentucky. The Kettle River potters kept churning out "Indian" pottery until 2001, when the plant closed. Now, the molds that used to fashion the vases, bowls, and other Nemadji clay items are dumped in a heap behind the building. Today, Nemadji pottery, especially vintage pieces, is a much-sought collector's item, the pots and vases lining antique shop shelves. Not bad for a company that based its business on the marketing of a myth.

WILLOW RIVER RUTABAGA PLANT

61 When one thinks of candidates for the National Register of Historic Places, a rutabaga warehouse and processing plant in Willow River does not necessarily leap to mind. However, the large concrete-block building off old Highway 61 can lay claim to that historic designation. It was built in 1935 alongside the former Northern Pacific Railroad right-of-way in the heart of Willow River. Historians say the warehouse is significant as Minnesota's only known example of a facility designed strictly for the storage and processing of the lowly rutabaga. Rutabagas and potatoes were once big cash crops in central and northern Pine County.

In the late nineteenth and early twentieth centuries, timber companies clearcut the region. When the remaining stumps, brush, and boulders were removed, the resulting landscape offered the right kind of sandy soil for root crops like rutabagas. This cousin to the turnip ruled that part of Pine County's agriculture for decades. By the 1950s, area farmers were growing three thousand tons of rutabagas each year, about one-fourth of the overall U.S. crop. Nearby Askov started calling itself the Rutabaga Capital of America.

There were several 'baga warehouses, but the Willow River facility is the only one that remains. Built by local Sven Anderson, it boasted mechanized handling, sorting, and processing equipment, much of which remains intact today. The process was fairly simple. Farmers unloaded the rutabagas into a "trap," a small, ground-level opening in the side of the building. The vegetables bounced through on a series of conveyor belts, were hand screened for quality, and then were sent to a processing room, where the roots were washed and dried and dipped into vats of hot wax to seal in freshness. Fire was always a threat because of the hot wax; in fact, two

The Willow River rutabaga plant, currently vacant

earlier Willow River warehouses were destroyed by blazes that started near the vats. After the 'bagas cooled, they were bundled into fifty-pound sacks and loaded onto railroad cars.

The Willow River rutabaga warehouse closed in 1955, but its National Register designation ensures its preservation. And pride in the past reigns as the city of Askov continues to celebrate the vegetable during an annual summer festival.

SANDSTONE "61"

Not much was required to make a traveler happy in the early days of highway road trips. A clean bed was a must. A hot shower was appreciated, even if the bathroom was tiny. And if you stayed in a motel with color TV in the 1960s, well, that was a swanky place indeed.

The "61" Motel in Sandstone was probably considered a pretty modern motel for its time. Not terribly fancy, but nice. It had a great location, right off busy Highway 61 as motorists entered town from the north.

In the early days, city visitors couldn't have missed the three-story Sandstone Hotel with its wide second-floor porch and "SANDSTONE HOTEL" painted on the front in big capital letters. But as times changed, so did accommodations. Before the "61" Motel, visitors to Sandstone could have stayed in one of the popular but rustic auto camps that offered a level piece of ground or wood platform for a tent.

Sandstone Hotel, ca. 1887

Perhaps motorists who wanted to call it a day could have stayed in a tiny tourist cottage, much like the ones along the North Shore.

Design of the first motel is credited to California architect Arthur Heineman, whose "Milestone Mo-Tel" (later the Motel Inn) was built in 1925 in San Luis Obispo, California. The white stucco, Spanish Mission–style bungalows had small kitchens and private garages and offered "every comfort and convenience of a first class hotel" for about $1.25 a day. All units faced a courtyard with a swimming pool and picnic tables. Confused travelers who saw billboards for Heineman's Mo-Tel thought *Hotel* had been misspelled. The coinage was a hybrid of "motor hotel"—and a deliberate calculation on Heineman's part. Would Americans, who were just beginning to taste the freedom offered by automobiles and starting to travel by car, welcome such accommodations? The answer was a resounding "yes." By 1929, one of the earliest motel chains was established in Waco, Texas. The Alamo Plaza Hotel Courts were the first examples of standardized accommoda-

The Sandstone "61"

tions for highway travelers: guests knew what they'd see when they turned the key to their room.

A 1933 edition of *The Architectural Record* noted that the construction of auto courts "has been the single growing and highly active division of the building in-dustry"—this at the height of the Great Depression. Early motels were very popu-lar, but some attracted less-than-savory guests, sparking a 1940 article in *American Magazine* called "Camps of Crime," with FBI director J. Edgar Hoover labeling problem auto courts "a new home of crime in America, a new home of disease, bribery, corruption, crookedness, rape, white slavery, thievery and murder." Yet most motels were run by concerned owners who lived on site and operated the business on a small, independent basis.

There is something special about staying in a motel that is a bit of a throwback to an earlier time. The "61" in Sandstone fits the bill. Its vintage neon sign sputters to life at dusk, beckoning travelers to call it a night—as it has since 1952.

THE GREAT HINCKLEY FIRE

Twenty-four years before the 1918 Moose Lake and Cloquet forest fires took place, another equally horrific blaze destroyed the town of Hinckley and several surrounding communities. The summer of 1894 was a dry one. Creeks, ponds, and lakes near Hinckley were low on water, and while people took notice, there were other things to worry about in a growing town of more than twelve hundred people. Hinckley, the financial center of Pine County, had two rail-roads, a lumber mill, five hotels, and many other thriving businesses.

September 1, 1894, was a hot day, one of many that dry summer. People in Hinck-

Hinckley after fire, 1894

ley had much to look forward to: Sunday was a day of rest after church services; Monday would be the first day of school; and on Tuesday the first national holiday of its kind was to be celebrated—Labor Day.

The trouble began with small brush fires burning near Beroun and Quamba about seven miles south and west of Hinckley. The flames slowly inched north. By early afternoon, the winds picked up and the fires started gaining strength and moving faster until they were just a few miles away from Hinckley. Residents began noticing that the sun had taken on a hazy cast and ash was drifting down from the sky. Two columns of smoke were marching toward town. The closer the columns came, the darker the sky became, until people were forced to light candles and kerosene lamps.

Survivors say the winds were blowing hard, sending smoke, dust, and ash through the streets. Some residents packed belongings and made their way to the depot to catch the 2:00 train out of town. Crews attempted to set up a firebreak to hold the advancing wall of flames, but by 3 or 3:30 PM, it became clear that the battle was hopelessly lost. Firefighters initially heard a deep roar and felt incinerator-like blasts of heat before they gave up and ran for their lives. In town, people tried to board a train from the Eastern Minnesota Railway while scores of others sought to leave on foot or by horse and wagon.

Huge waves of flames rolled into Hinckley, fanned by fierce winds created by the fire itself. Eyewitnesses saw tornadoes of fire spinning out of the wall, torching whatever lay in their path. The smoke and heat were unbearable. One of the heroes of that awful day was Eastern Minnesota engineer Bill Best, who patiently held the train so hundreds could climb aboard. He backed out of town and headed to Sandstone. In later accounts, passengers said they would never forget seeing people, some with their hair and clothes on fire, chasing the departing train.

Another train, from the St. Paul and Duluth Railroad, met droves of panicked settlers stumbling down the tracks, some half naked, their clothes having caught fire, and many covered in soot. Engineer James Root stopped to pick up about two hundred people and then set the train in reverse, only to become engulfed in flames. Somehow he managed to travel five miles to a lake, where the cars were evacuated and passengers told to leap into the muddy water to save themselves. They floated in Skunk Lake for hours, watching waves of flames rush over them.

Monument to the victims of the great Hinckley fire, dedicated in 1900

More than four hundred people died that day, although historians think the actual death toll was probably twice that number. Identifying many of the dead was nearly impossible because the corpses, some with nothing but shoes on their feet, were burned beyond recognition. Very little was left of Hinckley itself, as noted by the hordes of reporters who descended on the ruins in the days after the fire. The *Duluth News Tribune* called it a "Hamlet of Horrors."

Today, driving into Hinckley from the north on old Highway 61, motorists see a roadside marker that gives a bare-bones account of the 1894 fire. The whole gut-wrenching story is told in the Hinckley Fire Museum, located down the highway in the old Northern Pacific depot. Not far away, east of I-35 on Minnesota Highway 48, stands a towering stone monument that guards the graves of 248 Hinckley fire victims. Whole families rest in eternity together underneath four long, low mounds of earth. According to Daniel James Brown's excellent book, *Under a Flaming Sky*, an estimated two thousand people were caught in the fire. The hundreds who survived had amazing stories to tell. The last of their number died in 1996. Ann Anderson Darling was 102.

TOBIE'S

One of the best-known stops between the Twin Cities and Duluth is Tobie's Restaurant and Bakery. The original Tobie's was a two-story building with a big white awning on the corner of Main Street and Highway 61 in downtown Hinckley. It was a perfect spot for road-weary travelers to stop and get a cup of coffee and a little something to eat.

Most small towns have at least one cafe, and Isodore Wendt and his family opened theirs in 1920 to serve coffee and doughnuts, catering to customers who'd come in on the Greyhound bus. The Wendts ran the cafe for more than twenty-five years, until they sold it to Tobie Lackner and his wife in 1948. The sign out front was quickly changed to "Tobie's Eat Shop and Bus Stop."

The original Tobie's (ca. 1950) was on old Highway 61 in downtown Hinckley.

Tobie was a one-man PR agency for his little cafe. According to the current owners, he was fond of saying "early to bed, early to rise, work like hell and advertise." Tobie was a familiar face at big Twin Cities events like the state high school boys' basketball tournament, where he'd sponsor a hospitality suite every year. A colorful and gregarious man, Tobie decided to retire in 1966 because he realized the new freeway being built a few miles outside of town meant he'd have to move the cafe off Main Street in order to survive. The Schrade family bought the business, building a new restaurant along Interstate 35 but retaining the name.

Tobie's now includes a twenty-four-hour restaurant, gas station, bar, bakery, and gift shop and employs some two hundred people during the busy summer months. Just as baked goods were the big attraction at the cafe's original location on old Highway 61, the bakery and its famous rolls, sticky with gooey caramel or cinnamon sugar, bring in many travelers. Second- and third-generation family members now run the Hinckley landmark; they have no plans to give up the tradition that is Tobie's.

TOBIE'S USES MORE THAN FIVE THOUSAND GALLONS OF CARAMEL A YEAR FOR ITS CARAMEL AND CINNAMON ROLLS.

GRANT HOUSE

61 Like many small rural towns, Rush City grew up alongside a set of railroad tracks. The town was platted in 1870 by the Western Land Association, a subsidiary of the Lake Superior and Mississippi Railroad Company, which later became the St. Paul and Duluth Railroad. This first rail link between Duluth and the Minneapolis–St. Paul area ushered in a period of rapid growth for Rush City.

In fact, the town grew so quickly that there was a persistent housing shortage. In the early years, several hotels sprang up to shelter newcomers and rail passengers. One was the Grant House, built in 1880 by Colonel R. H. Grant, a distant cousin to the Civil War general and later president Ulysses S. Grant. R. H. Grant was no stranger to running a hotel, having done so in Hinckley before heading south to Rush City. The original Grant House—a spacious building with wide porches and carved bric-a-brac—developed a reputation as "the finest and most widely known hostelry on the St. Paul and Duluth road." It burned to the ground in 1895.

Undeterred, Colonel Grant rebuilt on the same site, using brick the second time around, and the "new" Grant House opened one year after the fire. Incidentally, that year, 1896, was a pretty exciting one in Minnesota: in May, ground was broken for the state capitol building, and later that month the St. Paul Saints professional baseball team played their first home game. In Rush City, the big news was the grand reopening of the Grant House.

The Grant House, 1918

Today the Grant House appears to be empty and for sale.

The Grant House served as a headquarters for traveling salesmen in the late 1800s and early 1900s: they set up in a "sample room" and sold their wares. One of the hotel's owners, the Challeen family, evidently entertained the traveling men by putting on boxing matches in the evenings.

Rush City's growth leveled off in the twentieth century, but the Grant House remains a local landmark. Today's travelers may wonder why the Grant House is included in a book that celebrates sites along Highway 61. Indeed, U.S. Highway 61 once traveled through Rush City on its way south to the Twin Cities. Today it becomes State Highway 361 shortly after leaving Pine City and remains 361 into Rush City, where it becomes County Road 30 through Chisago County until Wyoming, where it is once again designated as State Highway 61. The confusing change in route numbers and county/state designation can be chalked up to Interstate 35, which runs roughly parallel to the original path of Highway 61 from St. Paul to Duluth. Because I-35 was built to replace 61 as a main artery, the state transferred maintenance and jurisdiction of the old roadway to the applicable counties. The transfer of Highway 61 to Pine County occurred in 1966, and that stretch of road became known as Pine County 61. In Carlton County, the transfer occurred in 1971. Chisago County inherited 61 in 1970, after I-35 was completed. How did Highway 61 become Chisago County Road 30? Even county highway engineers are stumped. Maybe it just seemed like a nice round number.

OLD RUSH CITY FERRY

61 Travelers on old Highway 61 in Rush City who wanted to cross into Wisconsin would head east and drive a short distance down a gravel road. The road didn't end on the banks of the St. Croix River: it kept going courtesy the Rush City ferry.

From 1852 to about 1954 there were only two bridges across the St. Croix River but six ferries that moved between Minnesota and Wisconsin—at places like Soderbeck's Landing outside Pine City, Rush City, Sunrise, Amador, and Franconia. The ferries were established by smart businessmen who wanted to get farmers' crops to markets on either side of the river. Sometimes the growers themselves banded together to establish a ferry if none was available, as was the case on the Wisconsin side of the St. Croix in an area known as Evergreen. Farmers there bought shares to start a ferry to haul their grain to tiny Sunrise, Minnesota. The landing is still near the mouth of the Sunrise River in what is now Wild River State Park.

The wooden ferries could hold as many as four vehicles, or six on the larger boats. Magnus Soderbeck, owner of the Pine City ferry, carried the Ringling Brothers circus across the river on a couple of occasions. The Pine City newspaper published Soderbeck's description of the process: it looked a little like Noah's Ark as

Minnesota landing, Rush City ferry, 1931

the animals were led up the ramp and onto the boat. The elephants were another story, however: they had to wade across a shallow part of the river.

The Pine City and Rush City ferry crossings and others up and down the St. Croix could be very busy places, especially on weekends or holidays, when it wasn't unusual to ferry across as many as one hundred vehicles. In the 1930s, at twenty-five cents per crossing, ferry operators made decent money. The rates increased to fifty cents after World War II. The operators, who usually lived in small nearby cabins called "ferry houses," were on call twenty-four hours a day, seven days a week. In the dead of night, Rush City's Bill Mason dreaded hearing a car horn honking—the signal that someone needed to cross the river.

Bootleggers were frequent customers at ferry crossings, especially during Prohibition. Isolated wooded spots on the Wisconsin side of the river yielded good hiding places to make moonshine to ferry across for sale in Minnesota. Sometimes bootleggers would cross three or four times a night with hooch hidden in their cars. The ferry operators knew it, but they didn't ask questions so long as the fare got paid. Ferry landings were also prime places to party. Pine City residents remembered Soderbeck's Landing on the Fourth of July looking like the county fairgrounds some years, with people picnicking and playing games and taking the ferry across the river, only to turn around and come back.

Wooden footings for the ferry mechanism, visible in the water to the left

The Rush City ferry was at the end of the cleverly named Ferry Road. A cable stretched across the river to guide the boat: chains from its sides were attached to the cable with pulleys. After the gangplanks or aprons were pulled up, the ferry was launched at an angle, guided by the cables and using the current to propel it across. As the ferry moved closer to the opposite riverbank, operators used long poles to line up the boat with the landing. After awhile, ferries became motorized: Bill Mason's Rush City ferry had eight paddles attached to tire rims powered by a motor.

Visitors to the old Rush City ferry site on the St. Croix River can still see the footings for the wooden breakwater or dock that marked the landing site and allowed passengers to drive onto the ferry. Once abuzz with activity, the landings at Rush City, Pine City, and Sunrise are now only sites on a canoeist's map.

61 MINNESOTA The building that housed Carpenter's feed mill and grocery store shuddered a bit every time a Northern Pacific train rumbled through town, which was several times a day. The store was built by Joseph Carpenter in 1891 to serve the village of Oneka, which later became the town of Hugo.

Hugo was a small town with big dreams: its commercial club's motto was "America First—Hugo Next." Carpenter was vice president of the club, which according to its bylaws met at Carpenter's store on the first and third Mondays of the month, except during the height of summer—June, July, August, and September. New issues brought before the membership fell under several headings, including "health and hygiene," "patriotism," "industries and commerce," and "social affairs."

Carpenter's son, Frank, added to the category of "social affairs" in Hugo when he took over the business from his father in 1902 and added a dance hall and saloon. Frank Carpenter put the city on the map by sponsoring the Hugo town ball club, a semi-pro baseball team that was so good it drew as many as five hundred people for Sunday games. Players competed in a ball field across from Carpenter's and used the dance hall as a locker room. The team once made headlines by playing the mighty St. Paul Saints in Hugo.

Carpenter's Steakhouse

Frank sold the business in 1922, and a succession of owners followed. Carpenter's was a rollicking place in the thirties and forties: residents described it as a "little Las Vegas," with gambling, drinking, and dancing. A restaurant was added, and Carpenter's earned a reputation for excellent steaks. The old building, which has seen so much activity over its more than one-hundred-year history, will be demolished by 2009, and a new Carpenter's Steakhouse will be built just behind the old building, on Egg Lake. The bar's old tin ceiling and some mementoes will make the trip, but the rest of the building will become a piece of Hugo's past.

61

The modest white stucco building isn't fancy, but it has been holding a secret for decades. Its utilitarian look is the result of extensive remodeling, yet the White Bear Lake Township Hall can claim an impressive beginning.

Architectural historian Paul Clifford Larson was one of the few who knew the tiny township hall had been designed by noted architect Cass Gilbert. Gilbert gained national recognition in 1895 for his breathtaking vision and renderings of the Minnesota State Capitol. He went on to design the U.S. Supreme Court building in Washington, DC, as well as a number of graceful Summit Avenue mansions and several churches in St. Paul and the F. W. Woolworth Company Building in New York City, a precursor to modern-day skyscrapers.

Gilbert was not a Minnesota native. He and his family arrived in St. Paul when Cass was eight years old. His father, a surveyor for the U.S. Coast Survey, was in poor health, which he hoped would improve upon moving to Minnesota. He died in 1868. Cass stayed in Minnesota and, as a teenager, worked for a short time on a surveying crew for the Hudson and River Falls Railroad in Wisconsin. He studied

Voters at White Bear Town Hall, 1957

at the Massachusetts Institute of Technology but stayed there only a year. Instead, he went off to Europe and filled notebooks and sketchbooks with drawings of architectural details and building outlines. That experience helped secure him a spot at the prestigious firm of McKim, Mead and White, designers of many well-known public buildings including the Brooklyn Museum, the Minneapolis Institute of Arts, and the East and West Wings of the White House. But that job didn't last long.

Gilbert began honing his Minnesota connections and contacts. He hobnobbed with the wealthy, especially those who had—or wanted to have—summer homes in the White Bear Lake area, a fashionable vacation spot at the time. Gilbert designed at least a dozen White Bear summer cottages and a number of other smaller buildings, plugging away until his big break in 1895, when he won the state capitol design competition.

Thinking of Gilbert's more elaborate and elegant designs, it may seem odd that he created the nondescript White Bear Town Hall, which looks nothing like his later work. However, Larson points to a November 1885 building trades magazine for proof of the building's lineage. The *Inland Architect and Builder* reported that the twenty-six-year-old Gilbert had been given the assignment of designing the White Bear Town Hall. The fee: one thousand dollars.

Despite heavy remodeling in the 1970s, '80s, and '90s, the building retains hints of the hallmarks typical of Cass Gilbert designs. Underneath the 1920s-era stucco are vestiges of the original wood shingle and drop siding exterior. Echoes of Gilbert appear in the sweep of the building's eaves. He had a sharp eye for detail and was a stickler for careful craftsmanship.

The White Bear Town Hall, currently on Hoffman Road, part of Highway 61's original alignment

Not only has the town hall endured several remodelings, it has been moved many times, always in the vicinity of Highway 61. Its original site was on a spit of land between Goose and White Bear lakes. Plans are afoot to move the old hall a final time and restore it to what Cass Gilbert had in mind when he drafted the design in 1885. No matter how many cosmetic and structural changes or travels the White Bear Lake Township Hall has undertaken, one hopes it will always remain true to its original purpose: a place to do the people's work.

JUST OFF HIGHWAY 61 IN WHITE BEAR LAKE, WHERE THE PUBLIC BOAT LAUNCH IS NOW, THE ARCHITEC- TURALLY IMPRESSIVE RAMALEY'S PAVILION ONCE STOOD. BUILT IN 1890, THE PAVILION CATERED TO LAKE- SIDE GUESTS WHO ENJOYED ITS MANY CONCERTS, DANCES, AND MINSTREL SHOWS.

How is it that a Norwegian immigrant from White Bear Lake changed the entire course of sailboat racing on inland lakes? The answer lies along Highway 61 in a structure that once housed the Johnson Boatworks. The sprawling building is sandwiched between the highway and the shores of White Bear Lake.

The boatworks was started in 1896 by John O. Johnson. Upon arriving in this country from Norway at age eighteen, Johan Otto Johansen Americanized his name, settled into the White Bear community, and studied the craft of boat build- ing. As it turned out, his pursuit would prove both lucrative and historic.

In the 1880s, White Bear Lake was one of the best-known vacation spots in the Midwest. More than twenty-five passenger trains stopped there every day, as did streetcars by the dozens. The area was home to several large resorts, a pavilion for dancing and entertainment, and Wildwood Amusement Park. The lake was the fo- cal point around which centered all activities—including sailing. Along with Lake Minnetonka outside of Minneapolis, White Bear Lake was a prime spot for sailing, especially for the well-to-do with their sleek and expensive yachts. The White Bear Lake Yacht Club held races that usually prompted intense competition and much local newspaper coverage.

The old Johnson Boatworks fronting White Bear Lake, still used for boat storage

In his workshop, Johnson had been tinkering with a radical new boat design. Whereas traditional inland sailboats had deep hulls and heavy fixed keels to han- dle rougher water, Johnson designed one that would glide over the surface of the lake instead of plowing through it. The boat was lightweight and flat bottomed and had a rounded bow. Some sailors called it a "scow," a word used for garbage barges, because of its unusually flat de- sign. Wealthy sailing enthusiast C. Milton Griggs was intrigued with Johnson's odd boat, and he financed construction of another for the 1900 sailing season.

Sailors joked about the thirty-eight-foot-long boat looking like a "floating pan- cake." She was sleek and narrow, and Johnson knew from the first race that she was going to be fast. Indeed she was. Johnson recalled, "They sure were quiet when the race was over. We finished a mile ahead of the second place boat."

After that first, head-turning race, Captain Griggs dubbed the sailing scow the *Minnezitka,* a Native American word for "water bird." Griggs went on to win the White Bear Lake Yacht Club championship that year, and orders for the Johnson racing scow started coming in. With his boatworks in full production, John O. Johnson became nationally known as a top-notch boat designer. The *Minnezitka*'s design was so revolutionary that a model of the vessel is now part of the Smithsonian Institution's collection. She was the precursor to the "A" class of racing sailboats that can go as fast as fifteen to twenty miles an hour in a good wind.

A book written by Johnson's grandson, John W. Johnson, tells about the boatworks making thirty-two-foot class "B" sailboats for racing. Minnesota sailors carried home more than trophies: during Prohibition, the yachts *Freebooter* and the *Bootlegger* sailed in Canada and came back winners and also loaded down with illegal liquor. Over the years Johnson Boatworks churned out countless inland lake scows in assorted sizes. The staff built as many as one hundred handcrafted wooden boats each year and doubled production when they switched to fiberglass vessels.

John O. Johnson with a model of the Minnezitka

John O. Johnson was not only a gifted boat builder and designer, he was also quite an inventor. Long smitten with the idea of flying, Johnson was one of the first Minnesotans to gain altitude using a motor-powered aircraft. The maiden flight took place in January 1910 and was covered by the *St. Paul Dispatch*. Johnson's aircraft had mammoth wings thirty feet long and eight feet wide. He managed to fly about twenty feet up in the air for a distance of about two hundred feet before the engine gave out. The spectacle caused quite a stir. Johnson recalled that as a lad on a Norwegian whaling ship he watched the bow wave, which gave him ideas for the shapes of boat hulls and airplane wings. He obviously put those ideas to good use.

After Johnson's death in 1963, the boatworks continued to operate until 1998. The boat molds were sold to Melges Boatworks in Wisconsin, and production ceased at the White Bear Lake facility. The lakefront property continues to be a home for sailors. No doubt John O. Johnson would approve.

One site along Highway 61 holds special significance in Minnesota broad-casting history and for this author in particular. In suburban Maplewood, in the midst of all the car dealerships, stands a brick building with an Art Deco facade and a huge radio tower looming behind it. It is the transmitter build-ing for KSTP-AM, a fifty-thousand-watt, clear channel radio station.

The station was founded—and is still locally owned—by the Hubbard family. Patriarch Stanley E. Hubbard was one of broadcasting's pioneers, the first to de-velop a commercial radio station, "commercial" in that it made money by selling on-air ads. WAMD—"Where All Minneapolis Dances," the slogan of the Marigold Ballroom—went on the air in 1923. The station set up shop in the ballroom, and Hubbard agreed to do live broadcasts of the bands that played there each night.

WAMD was destroyed by a fire in 1927. Undeterred, Hubbard applied for a li-cense for a new station. His plans were to broadcast from studios in the main lobby of the St. Paul Hotel. During a special ceremony in 1928, President Calvin Coolidge pressed a key in the White House and KSTP Radio went on the air in St. Paul.

KSTP radio transmitter under construction in 1936, Highway 61 visible at far right (courtesy KSTP-AM, LLC)

KSTP's call letters appear in a long list of broadcasting firsts. KSTP was the first station, in 1929, to use a portable transmitter to broadcast events. In 1930, Hubbard helped form the first national radio news service, with bureaus in Chi-cago, New York, the Twin Cities, and Washington, DC. KSTP also hosted some of the first appearances by soon-to-be entertainment superstars Jack Benny, the Marx Brothers, and Edgar Bergen.

In the 1930s, enjoying success upon success, Hubbard decided to build a state-of-the-art radio transmitter along Highway 61 in a swampy part of Maple-wood. Engineers thought the wetland would help sharpen the AM radio signal, offering better reception for listeners. They were right: the water grounded the towers and improved the way the signals traveled. In some cases the reception was so good that KSTP was heard aboard U.S. Navy ships during World War II—all the way out in the Pacific.

Hubbard and other radio pioneers realized early on the potential power of the new medium. Radio captured the imagination then, and it still does today: time has not dissolved its magical qualities. Early radio programs grabbed listeners by the ears and whisked them off to the swanky Marigold Ballroom or even to London, to experience wartime air raids. Listeners could "see" the Lone Ranger riding across the range or picture an exasperated George Burns as he traded quips with Gracie Allen. Radio connected Americans as they heard about the nation's travails, celebrated its triumphs, and shared in its sorrows. Radio was as predomi-

KSTP Radio

nant then as television is today: in the mid-1940s, more than eighty out of every one hundred people owned a radio. Yet change was inevitable, and Hubbard was one of the first to embrace the newest technology of the time: television. He set up a demonstration at the 1939 Minnesota State Fair, and in 1948 KSTP-TV went on the air.

KSTP-AM is still on the air. For a time, its staff was located at the transmitter site. It was a pretty tight fit: one of the salesmen would hit his head on the transmitter if he leaned back too far in his chair, and the newsroom was actually more of a hallway. I know because my first job as a reporter was with KSTP and Hubbard Broadcasting. To this day, I always smile whenever I drive past the transmitter towers of KSTP-AM Radio—even if I am listening to another station.

61 Highway 61 flows into East Seventh Street in St. Paul. This area, known as the Dayton's Bluff neighborhood, boasts a spectacular view of downtown, which provides an appropriate backdrop for a striking red brick building at East Seventh Street and Eichenwald. This structure has played any number of roles over its long life. As of 2008, the Ethiopian Evangelical Church of Minnesota calls it home, but it began as the Dayton's Bluff Commercial Club in 1905.

Commercial clubs were found all over the country in the nineteenth and well into the twentieth centuries. They were places where business and civic leaders could meet to discuss community issues, plan public activities, and relax a little. The Dayton's Bluff club was remodeled in 1913 to include bowling lanes, a locker room, a dance floor, a banquet hall, a billiard area, and a men's smoking room.

Dayton's Bluff Commercial Club, ca. 1920s

One of the commercial club's roles was as the neighborhood's chief public booster. A thirty-page booklet from 1909 entitled "Picturesque Dayton's Bluff" makes quite a sales pitch to prospective residents and businesspeople, waxing poetically about the area's growth, which is "strong and vigorous and adding force and character as the days go by." The booklet also gives a fair amount of credit to the prominent men of Dayton's Bluff, stating that "the wonderful strides in material progress made by this section of the city are largely due to the Commercial Club." Indeed, names like Hamm, Bremer, and Keller appeared among the club's membership; these men were some of the community's key decision makers.

Commercial club members involved themselves in a number of St. Paul civic celebrations as a way to call attention to the neighborhood. William Hamm, founder of Hamm's Brewery, helped organize the first St. Paul Winter Carnival in 1886. In subsequent years, the Dayton's Bluff community was represented with floats in the carnival parade, and in 1938 it was the site of an ice palace. The commercial club was also a hub of community activities—festivals and weddings, bowling league banquets and wrestling matches.

Dayton's Bluff Marching Club, St. Paul Winter Carnival, ca. 1939

In the 1930s, as Minnesota and the rest of the nation struggled through the Depression, the commercial club announced a push to bring new industries to Dayton's Bluff. At the time, the major employer was 3M's East Side facility. The club set up a "bureau of publicity" to launch the project. Also in the 1930s, cars became more important as a mode of transportation, changing the face of Seventh Street and the commercial club structure itself. The avenue was widened to make room for vehicle traffic, and the commercial club building lost its entryway and balcony during the renovation.

According to area historian Steve Trimble, in an article written for the Dayton's Bluff community newsletter, the focus of the commercial club shifted during and after World War II. Older members felt the club moved away from civic and economic issues and began emphasizing social concerns. Some believed the club had lost its leadership role, and in 1950 a new organization was established: the East Seventh Street Business Association. Today, other community organizations keep the neighborhood's interests in mind. But the old commercial club building, home in recent years to a new generation of organizations, attests to the belief that the Dayton's Bluff community had—and continues to have—much to offer.

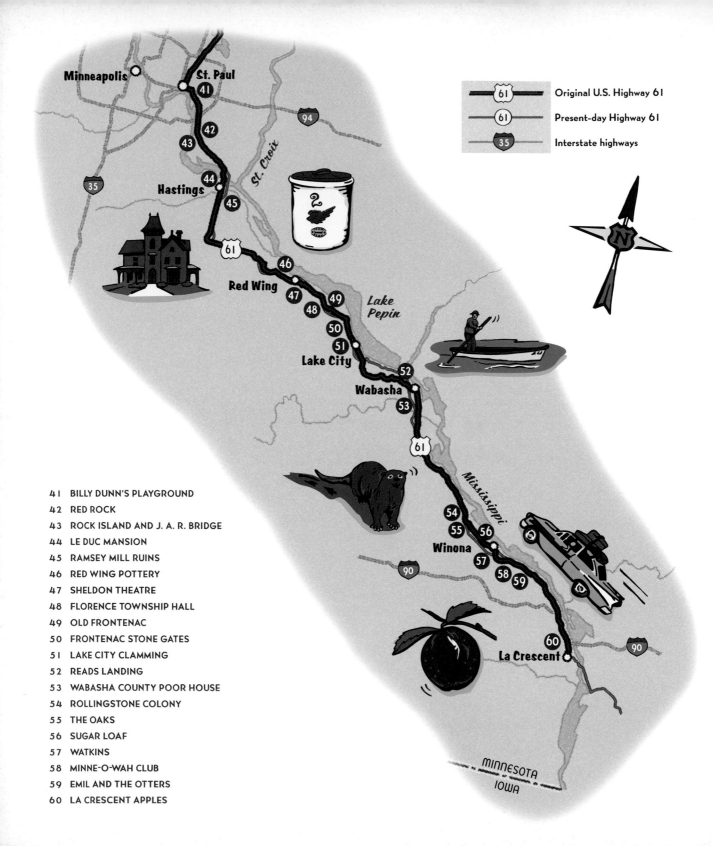

Minneapolis   St. Paul
41

42

43
94

St. Croix

44
Hastings
45

61
46
Red Wing
47 49
48   Lake Pepin
50
51
Lake City
52
Wabasha
53

61

Mississippi

54
55 56
Winona
57
58 59
90

60
La Crescent
90

MINNESOTA
IOWA

Original U.S. Highway 61   61
Present-day Highway 61   61
Interstate highways   35

N

LEIDEL'S ORCHARD

IN BUSINESS SINCE 1917

Bluff Country

61 There seem to be conflicting stories over an unusual site on Point Douglas Road, one of Highway 61's original pathways south of St. Paul. Not in dispute is what happened at what was Dunn's Service Station. For years, motorists along that busy stretch would stop at Dunn's for a fill-up and a check of their oil. On the morning of April 4, 1963, a Thursday, little Billy Dunn, a toddler about four years old, was helping his dad, Robert Dunn, and his grandpa, Cletus Dunn, pick up litter around the service station. A gasoline tanker truck arrived to deliver a load of fuel. It was a run-of-the-mill stop, and the driver chatted with the elder Dunns and little Billy as he poured gas into the storage tanks. He was getting ready to leave when someone noticed Billy was missing. Thinking the boy was safe inside the Dunns' nearby pickup truck, the driver slowly started to back out, only to hear a stomach-wrenching scream. He had accidentally backed over the little boy, killing him instantly. The accident merited a short front-page story in that afternoon's *St. Paul Dispatch*.

The Dunns didn't keep the service station open long after Billy's death. Family members were heartbroken, especially Grandpa Dunn. The old man had long grown grapes on a parcel of

above: Memorial or mini-golf course? Billy Dunn's playground, 1970s

right: Whatever the story, experts agree the pieces are interesting examples of roadside folk art.

land next to the service station. In the years after Billy's death, he added a menagerie of animals, and when the Queen Anne Kiddieland Amusement Park in Bloomington closed, the elder Dunn bought a treasure trove of life-sized storybook figures and a child-sized merry-go-round to add to his eclectic collection. Motorists likely mistook it for a miniature golf course, and maybe it was. The Ramsey County Historical Society survey of the site categorizes it as such, but a walk around the grounds today yields no sign of that kind of activity. Family members insist the statues meant something much more to Cletus Dunn.

Dunn's Service Station is now a used car lot. A battered elephant and a giant concrete snowman guard the forlorn-looking field. It isn't clear just why the quirky site fell into disrepair. Cletus Dunn died in 1975. If the strange congregation of statues was indeed Cletus's way of honoring his lost grandchild, then an empty wishing well stands in mute testament to a little boy who never had the chance to experience its magical powers and to a family who wished, daily, to bring him back. The true origin of the statues on Point Douglas Road remains one of history's mysteries.

RED ROCK

Not far off Highway 61 along the Mississippi River in Newport is a site now peppered with oil storage tanks and warehouses. This once lovely spot used to draw thousands of reverent Methodists for song, prayer, and praise; long before them, Native Americans came here for almost the same reasons. The place was called Red Rock, and there is quite a story behind it.

It begins, as it should, with the native inhabitants. The Dakota revered a large solitary granite rock found alongside the river, the only such boulder in the area. The rock's odd location led the Dakota to believe there must be great power associated with it: whatever force put the rock there should be respected and appreciated. In keeping with Dakota beliefs, the rock became a place of *wakan,* where the mysterious is honored. People from the nearby village of Kaposia decorated the rock with an ochre paint mix, carefully drawing stripes and other designs and leaving offerings of food, tobacco, and sacred items. The boulder became known as *Inyan Sa* or "Red Rock."

The first written account of Red Rock came in 1805, when explorer Zebulon Pike made note of a "large painted stone" about eight miles below the Dakota village. Methodist missionaries, sent to convert the Indians to Christianity, kept track of the many visits the Dakota paid to the site. Recognizing the rock's spiritual significance to the Indians, Reverend Benjamin Kavanaugh decided to move his mission to the east side of the Mississippi river, near Red Rock, in 1839. He constructed a few small buildings and established the first Protestant church for white settlers in the area.

Red Rock camp meeting,
ca. 1910

For years prior to missionaries' arrival in Minnesota, big outdoor religious revivals were held in the South. The "camp meetings" were several days of preaching, praying, and confessions where tens of thousands worshipped with unbridled abandon. Some participants were moved to bark or cry or faint during the proceedings. The partylike atmosphere attracted people who probably wouldn't have attended church but who seized the opportunity to accept the Lord, right there among the trees and the tents. During the mid- to late 1850s, camp meetings became more common throughout Minnesota, growing in size and popularity, but the biggest ones were to come at Red Rock.

The first camp meeting at this site took place in 1869, in late June and early July. A newspaper report indicated that some two thousand attendees clogged the grounds, along with tents and horses and wagons. It wasn't as raucous as the early southern camp meetings were, but it was lively by midwestern standards.

As Red Rock's popularity grew, so did attendance. One camp meeting in 1876 was said to have drawn "all creeds, colors and nationalities." The site's location close to St. Paul, with access to trains and steamboat landings, probably didn't hurt. A three-story hotel was built, as were cottages, a dining hall, and an open pavilion that seated about eighteen hundred people. Following those improvements, about ten thousand attended an 1883 meeting. Some reports indicate as many as thirty thousand people showed up when famous evangelists came to preach. The salvation of all those souls was exactly what the Red Rock Campgrounds Association had in mind when it wrote its mission statement around 1900: "The object of this Association is the advancement of the Kingdom of God among men; especially by the conversion of the unsaved and the promotion of that doctrine."

Camp meetings continued at Red Rock until 1938, when the camp and the rock were moved. The acres of campground were prime property for industrial development, and today very little remains of the natural environment that once was the Red Rock site. The rock itself was taken to a new Methodist Bible camp on Medicine Lake, outside downtown Minneapolis. Many adults may remember from their childhood similar church camps all around the region: perhaps they had their roots in the Red Rock experience. Before the move, the Dakota Indians had one last chance to paint Inyan Sa the way they had decades before.

Red Rock at its current home, in front of the Newport United Methodist Church

The Dakota still think of Red Rock as one of their important spiritual sites; the spot also holds significance for United Methodists. The church kept the rock, despite the Native American view that no man can "own" such a sacred piece of earth. The rock was moved back to the Newport area in 1964 but not to its original location. Instead, it and Reverend Kavanaugh's rebuilt cabin are on the grounds of the Newport United Methodist Church, on a bluff overlooking the original—and now much altered—Red Rock site.

ROCK ISLAND AND J. A. R. BRIDGE

61 For decades, motorists crossing the Mississippi River from St. Paul Park to Inver Grove Heights would occasionally do so with freight trains rumbling above their heads. Built in 1895 by the Pittsburgh Bridge Company for the venerable Rock Island Railroad, the bridge was unusual, one of the few of its kind over the Mississippi: a double-decker steel truss span that swung open in the middle to allow barges through. Trains ran on the top deck; cars on the bottom. The South St. Paul Beltline Railroad also used it to connect the South St. Paul stockyards with the main rail lines that ran through St. Paul Park.

The narrow Rock Island toll bridge offered barely enough room for two cars to pass (ca. 1934).

The span was built in the days before motorized traffic, so the narrow bridge deck was only about one and a half lanes wide. It must have made for a heart-stopping crossing as oncoming cars attempted to squeeze past one another. The Rock Island Railroad operated it as a toll bridge until 1938, when the Minnesota legislature dropped that provision and it became free to cross. But when the railroad went bankrupt and closed the bridge in 1980, a private businessman, Al Roman, and his wife, Joan, bought the span and started operating it as a toll bridge again, charging seventy-five cents per crossing.

The former J. A. R. Bridge

As it turns out, the J. A. R. (Joan and Al Roman) Bridge became the last toll bridge in the metro area. The decaying span began showing its age, and in 1999 an inspection found deficiencies too expensive to fix. The bridge was closed for safety reasons, and Washington County seized the property because the owners reportedly had failed to pay back taxes. When it closed, approximately two thousand vehicles were crossing the bridge every day.

Its useful life over, the J. A. R. Bridge was swung into the open position to accommodate river traffic and sat idle, becoming what one Washington County commissioner called "a pile of rusty junk." As late as 2005, the tollbooth was still in place, but the span was covered in graffiti and a fire set by vandals did some damage. The road to the bridge on the east side of the river, the Washington County side, is completely blocked off and security is tight because of a nearby oil refinery. The road is also blocked off on the Dakota County side, but that doesn't stop visitors. There is something intriguing about the old bridge that draws people to it, to walk along its length or to sit quietly on its concrete deck. Time has caught up with the J. A. R. Bridge, and while there are plans to tear down the Washington County section sometime in 2008, there is still some question as to what to do with the Dakota County side. Some people would like to see portions of it kept standing, perhaps as a fishing pier. Funding for such a venture, of course, remains a question mark.

LE DUC MANSION

61 The buff-colored limestone mansion that proudly stands on the corner of Seventeenth and Vermillion Streets in Hastings is among the most beautiful old homes on Highway 61. Certainly the *Hastings Independent* in 1864 thought it was "the nicest in the state."

The mansion was built by William Gates Le Duc and his wife, Mary. William was an energetic and optimistic young man from Ohio when he arrived in Minnesota Territory in July 1850. He found his destination of St. Paul to be "a straggling frontier town," but that less-than-charitable characterization didn't stop him from quickly launching his career in the city. He set up a law practice and a book and stationery store. He also invested in land, buying property in St. Paul, West St. Paul, and Hastings. Le Duc saw lucrative business opportunities in the river town of Hastings. He invested in the Hastings Ferry Company, developed and owned a flour mill on the nearby Vermillion River, and obtained a charter for the Hastings and Dakota Railroad Company. He also owned two farms close to town and a parcel of land not far from the falls of the Vermillion River and his mill.

The ambitious Le Duc had great dreams, and he intended to build an opulent home symbolic of the station in life he hoped to achieve. In setting their sights high, the Le Ducs kept with social conventions of the Victorian Era. Refinement and gentility were heavily endorsed in scores of publications written by etiquette advisors and style mavens. Magazines and books dictated self-improvement in a number of areas, including dress, mannerisms, taste, and even proper leisure time activities. The message was clear: even if one wasn't well bred, one could act the part. The emphasis on taste and style was also seen in the writings and philosophy of landscape architect Andrew Jackson Downing, who promoted the ideals of cultural refinement as they related to architecture and the surrounding natural environment.

ONE OF THE MOST INTERESTING BRIDGES BUILT IN MINNESOTA WAS THE SPIRAL BRIDGE IN HASTINGS. THE IDEA WAS TO FUNNEL TRAVELERS INTO THE DOWNTOWN RIVERFRONT AREA WITH A GRADUAL SPIRAL DESCENT INSTEAD OF USING A TRADITIONAL BRIDGE DESIGN THAT, ALTHOUGH A STRAIGHT SHOT ACROSS THE RIVER, WOULD DEPOSIT TRAFFIC A FEW BLOCKS OFF OF MAIN STREET. THE SPIRAL BRIDGE BECAME A HASTINGS LANDMARK BUT, IN THE FACE OF HEAVY MODERN-DAY CAR AND TRUCK TRAFFIC, WAS DISMANTLED IN 1951.

The Le Duc mansion was based on sketches in Downing's guidebook *Cottage Residences*. It was going to be lovely, and the Le Ducs were excited about their dream home. But there was one major problem: William Le Duc never had a lot of money. He was always just one dream away from making a lucrative business deal, never quite hitting the mark. The original budget for the mansion was two thousand dollars. Contractors upped the amount to five thousand dollars, and the bills kept mounting as work slowly progressed from 1862 to 1865. During that time Le Duc went off to fight for the Union Army in the Civil War, becoming a captain and distinguishing himself in several battles. His Civil War record may have been stellar, but his finances were not. He wrote to Mary in 1863 that he realized it would take all that he could earn and cash from a good harvest to pay off the construction debt. Actually, much more would be required: the final bill for the house and surrounding buildings was almost thirty thousand dollars.

The Le Duc children at home, 1894

A tour of the Le Duc mansion today finds very little furniture and certainly nothing terribly expensive or elegant. Le Duc's accumulated debt kept the family from buying the kind of furnishings Mary longed for. Instead, the pieces inside the grand fifteen-room mansion consisted of simple family hand-me-downs and heirlooms.

Still, the family led lives rich in educational and creative pursuits. William became a gentleman farmer and an excellent horticulturist. He experimented with fruit trees and planted hundreds of seedlings around Hastings. His interest in horticulture turned out to be quite useful: in 1877 he was appointed U.S. commissioner of agriculture in the administration of President Rutherford B. Hayes, an old Civil War buddy. Hayes even paid a visit to Hastings, staying at the Le Duc mansion in September 1878. Unfortunately, Le Duc was not reappointed to the position in 1881, and the family returned to Hastings. Several years later, Le Duc's daughters Florence and Alice ran a needlework business out of the mansion. Le Duc made Hastings his home until he died in 1917 at the ripe age of ninety-five. His children used the old mansion as a summer home for many years and later sold it to a family friend who used it as an antique shop until the mid-1980s.

Le Duc Mansion

The mansion with its brick red trim sat empty for many years behind its wrought iron gates, its peaked tower fostering the impression of a haunted house in some old horror movie. Then it was donated to the Minnesota Historical Society, and an extensive remodeling effort ensures that the Le Duc mansion will be preserved for generations, looking much as it did when the family lived there. The city of Hastings now owns the mansion, and the Dakota County Historical Society operates it as a museum, keeping alive the story of one very intriguing gentleman, William Gates Le Duc.

RAMSEY MILL RUINS

61 One of William Le Duc's business ventures was a mill located just around the corner from his mansion, along the nearby Vermillion River. Still in use, it is one of the oldest continuously operating mills in the state. It survived when several others on the Vermillion did not, including the Ramsey Mill.

Its namesake, Alexander Ramsey, was appointed the first governor of Minnesota Territory, a post he held until 1853. Ramsey was trained as a lawyer, but after leaving office he all but abandoned his practice to focus on Minnesota real estate investments—a lucrative move, as it turned out.

In 1857, Ramsey and a friend, Dr. Thomas Foster, teamed up to buy land on the lower falls of the Vermillion River in Hastings. William Le Duc was also interested in the property, but evidently he couldn't make the mortgage or interest payments. The Ramsey group built a mill of stone three stories high and filled with the very latest in milling technology. Instead of traditional millstones for crushing kernels of wheat, the Ramsey Mill boasted rollers, a brand-new method that would be used for decades to come. The mill produced Belle of Hastings flour, one hundred barrels a day when operating at full tilt.

above: Ramsey Mill, ca. 1865

right: Mill ruins from an overlook downstream

The same year he launched his milling operation, Ramsey joined the newly formed Republican Party. He ran for governor in 1858 and lost, but he was successful in his bid two years later, becoming the second elected governor of the state of Minnesota. Then, in 1863, the state legislature sent him to the U.S. Senate. He sold the Ramsey Mill in Hastings several years later.

After changing hands a few times, the mill went up in a spectacular fire on the cold night of December 22, 1894. The *Hastings Gazette* reported a week later that a south wind had fanned the fire and "before the [fire] department reached the building, it was enveloped in flames and nothing could be saved." Everything was destroyed, from five hundred bushels of wheat and several hundred barrels of flour to the mill's accounting ledgers. The monetary damages were staggering for the era—twelve to fifteen thousand dollars, with no insurance. The mill was never rebuilt. The slowly decaying ruins still stand along the riverbank, now offering a focal point for Hastings's Mill Ruins Park.

61 Motorists heading south into Red Wing on Highway 61 could see one of the city's landmarks from quite a distance. It was hard to miss the huge "POTTERY SALESROOM" sign looming over the low-slung building. The sign is still there, as is the sturdy brick pottery factory, but the business known as Red Wing Potteries, Inc., is not. The factory that churned out everything from stoneware crocks and spittoons to ceramic ashtrays and dinnerware closed in 1967.

Red Wing's entry into the pottery business can be traced to a German immigrant by the name of John Paul. In 1861 he discovered that local clay could be used to make stoneware, and the industrious potter soon began selling his creations to neighbors.

From that modest start, Red Wing became home to several companies that made distinctively marked stoneware crocks, jugs, and churns from the 1880s through the 1940s. The thick-walled containers, some holding as many as sixty gallons, were the Tupperware of their time, used for storing meat and butter and other foods since refrigeration often wasn't available. These pieces were finished with a salt glaze that gave the containers a tannish color and a distinctive dimpled surface. The salt glaze also sealed the vessel to keep it from leaking.

Clay for the stoneware came from a rich vein located a few miles outside town in a little place appropriately named Claybank. A lower grade of clay from the same area was used to make sewer pipe. Between crews digging out the clay and shipping it to Red Wing and hundreds of workers fashioning products out of the clammy, compacted soil, the city became the pottery capital of the Midwest.

Farmers were big buyers of Red Wing stoneware, but as more of them acquired refrigerators the market dropped off in the 1920s. To diversify its offerings, the Red Wing Union Stoneware Company started producing flowerpots and then artistically made pottery like vases, ashtrays, cookie jars, mugs, and other items. The company also made distinctive dinnerware, which drew a lot of attention. By 1936, so little stoneware was made that the company changed its name to Red Wing Potteries, Inc., and focused on dinnerware and art pottery pieces that are much sought after even today.

At the height of its business, in the 1940s, Red Wing Potteries employed approximately three hundred workers. Some, like Virginia Lewellen, remember the radiating heat of the pottery factory: she and her colleagues were stationed close to kilns operating at full blast. In an oral history for the Goodhue County Historical Society, Virginia said cooling fans were not allowed in the manufacturing department because the damp clay pieces would crack if they dried too quickly. Virginia's job was trimming teapots as they came out of their molds, making sure to smooth out any ridges or seams.

Most of the artists who patiently sat and painted the designs on Red Wing Potteries dinnerware were women. Originally, only two women did all the hand painting, but eventually as many as ninety wielded paintbrushes. Each woman would paint specific colors using a specific brushstroke on a specific pattern. The patterns changed daily, as did the items, depending on the production schedule. Still, it was painstaking, tedious work. Marion Bjorklund, who worked at the pottery in the 1940s, remembered in a 2001 oral history how hard it was to master the technique: "The first three days I practiced and they threw everything away. When I got the hang of painting, then you started right in. I painted green leaves for quite awhile, and later on, the other parts. And the roses! When I got to them, that was the hardest thing I think to paint!"

above: The decorating department at Red Wing Pottery, ca. 1950

below: A familiar sight along Highway 61 in Red Wing, ca. 1958

Red Wing dinnerware enjoyed enormous popularity. It was sold across the country in some of the best department stores, but many Minnesota brides-to-be remember making a personal pilgrimage to the Red Wing Pottery salesroom off Highway 61 to pick out their dinnerware pattern. Maybe it was the snazzy "Smart Set"; perhaps the whimsical "Bob White" birds caught their fancy. By 1967, the showroom was earning receipts of $386,000, which accounted for nearly 25 percent of company sales.

Grave marker of Francis Olson, Oakwood Cemetery, Red Wing

Despite the popularity of their products, the potters themselves were largely unknown. They weren't allowed to sign their pieces, and so most worked in anonymity their entire career. But whether their daily task was to press clay into molds or trim the still-damp pieces or paint leaves on plates, some workers quietly unleashed their creativity at lunchtime. They took advantage of the company's clay, kilns, and paints and created stunning, fanciful, and heartfelt works to give as gifts or to commemorate special events. These one-of-a-kind "noon hour pieces" are incredibly rare and highly collectible today. Each has a story behind it—and that is also true of the poignant pieces handmade by some potters at the Red Wing Sewer Pipe Company. Many used their skills to create touching final tributes to loved ones. Several of the grave markers at the nearby Oakwood Cemetery, including many for children, are made of dark clay sewer pipe, each personally decorated and inscribed.

The last of the Red Wing pieces came out of the kilns in 1967. A labor strike, foreign competition, and an antiquated factory spelled the end of Red Wing Potteries after nearly one hundred years. The Red Wing Sewer Pipe Company lingered a while longer, closing its doors in the 1970s.

The pottery factory still stands off Highway 61, including the remnants of an old kiln near the parking lot. That kiln used to be nearly as long as the pottery factory itself, able to handle hundreds of pieces at a time. The manufacturing floors now house shops and restaurants, but the glory days aren't forgotten. A museum on the second floor tells the story of Red Wing pottery—what the business meant to the people of this city and what the crocks, dinnerware, and other collectibles still mean to those who appreciate their timeless beauty.

BEYOND POTTERY, THIS CITY IS KNOWN INTERNATIONALLY FOR SHOES: BOTH RED WING AND RIEDELL. RIEDELL HAS MADE ICE SKATES SINCE 1945, AND SOME OF THE MOST FAMOUS U.S. CHAMPIONS HAVE USED THE RED WING–MADE SKATES. FOUNDERS PAUL AND SOPHIE RIEDELL WERE PAIRS SKATERS, AND PAUL HAS BEEN INDUCTED INTO BOTH THE ICE- AND ROLLER-SKATING HALLS OF FAME.

61 From the intricate mosaic tile floor to the marble columns, the gilded lobby of the Sheldon Theatre is a feast for the eyes. With so much to look at, it is easy to miss the carved plaster birds with their outstretched wings stationed over the lobby doors. Without some background on the history of the Sheldon, it's also easy to miss their symbolism.

The curtain went up for the first time at the Sheldon Auditorium in 1904. The best seats in the house cost four dollars, but for some patrons it was worth the price to experience opening night in the first municipal theater in the United States. The benefactor, Theodore B. Sheldon, hadn't lived to see that first performance, dying four years earlier at the age of eighty. Sheldon was one of Red Wing's business leaders. He was a major player in the creation of the Minnesota Stoneware Company, which later became Red Wing Potteries. He had a hand in the Red Wing Gas, Light and Power Company, the Red Wing Furniture Company, the Duluth, Red Wing and Southern Railway, the La Grange mills, a bank, and a construction company. When Sheldon died, he left a sizable amount of money to be used on behalf of the city for the "education, enjoyment, improvement or amusement of the people of Red Wing." The trustees of his estate decided that a municipal theater would be a fine tribute to Sheldon and a lasting cultural gift to the city.

A "jewel box" of a theater

Early on, the Sheldon was described as a "jewel box" because of its gold and ivory embellishments, carved sconces, marble pillars, velvet curtains, and glittering tiered chandeliers. All these elegant flourishes went up in smoke when a fire started around 2 AM on February 22, 1918. Fire officials thought smoldering cigarette butts from a traveling troupe could have caused the blaze, which gutted the interior, causing more than forty thousand dollars in damage. Repairs were made and the theater reopened. Instead of a play that second opening night, a movie was shown. Movies were growing in popularity, and they were moneymakers, drawing an auditorium full of patrons, kids paying a dime and adults twenty cents. Compare that to the average ticket price for a play, which was $1.50.

A large-scale renovation in the 1930s updated the Sheldon into a movie house but removed the horseshoe-shaped balcony in order to seat more people. More ambitious renovations occurred in the 1960s, nearly obliterating the Sheldon's elegant charm. The gold leaf in the proscenium arch was painted over, as were the ceiling figures. Acoustic tiles were put up on the walls, and the imported damask coverings came down. Vinyl wallpaper, easy to clean but not very attractive, was pasted over stenciled designs. The Sheldon became just another bland movie theater.

Throughout the 1960s and '70s, the Sheldon Auditorium cost more money for upkeep than it earned in ticket sales. In the 1980s, Red Wing city leaders contemplated restoring the Sheldon to its former elegance and operating it as a live performing arts center, an idea that generated a lot of interest. Garrison Keillor of Minnesota Public Radio's popular program *A Prairie Home Companion* called wider public attention to the theater when he broadcast the show from the Sheldon. Community fundraising efforts were started, a city bond referendum passed, and the needed money was raised by the fall of 1986.

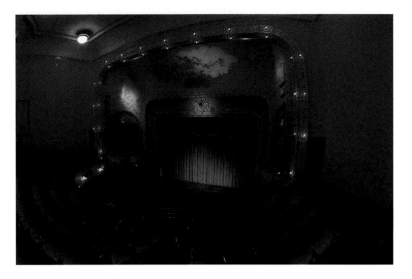

Sheldon Theatre auditorium

As a crowd of enthusiastic supporters gathered in the lobby to take a last look before construction began, however, a second fiery tragedy struck. When they moved into the theater, they were shocked and horrified to see flames shooting up by the stage. As people escaped to safety, there was a huge explosion. The resulting fire ruined the interior. Four million dollars later, the Sheldon, like the mythical phoenix, rose from the ashes, and it reopened on September 10, 1988, looking very much as it did when patrons first saw it in 1904.

The Sheldon now seats about five hundred people and plays host to an unknown number of spirits. The manager and some performers have reported odd happenings, like elevators moving when no one else is in the building or lights flickering at strange times. Maybe it's faulty wiring, but it could be the spirit of T. B. Sheldon making his presence known, pleased that his gift to Red Wing is still being enjoyed.

FLORENCE TOWNSHIP HALL

61 When elected officials meet in the historic Florence Town Hall, they conduct business just a few feet away from a raised stage with a painted canvas backdrop from 1918. Old-fashioned melodramas used to be staged in the town hall, some theatrical, some political. In fact, the fight to save the town hall was itself quite dramatic.

The Florence Town Hall has been the official seat of government for the township since 1875, making it the oldest continuously used town hall in Minnesota. The little white clapboard building was showing its age in the 1990s, and some residents proposed that it be torn down and government meetings and voting be held in a new community center instead. The fight over the township hall's future became heated and emotional. Those on one side, wanting a new community center, thought the township hall was too small and too expensive to renovate. Those in favor of restoring the historic building passionately argued that it was a part of the community's identity and needed to be saved. Those forces won. Indeed, the town hall is an important link to the area's past.

Land for the town hall was deeded to the Florence Township board for one dollar by General Israel Garrard in 1875. Garrard first arrived in the Frontenac area on a hunting trip with his brother in 1854 and was so impressed with the beautiful landscape and the potential for development that he stayed here while his brother returned to Ohio. Eventually the Garrard family became the driving force behind what is now Old Frontenac, a cluster of meticulously restored homes on a bluff overlooking Lake Pepin.

It was called simply Frontenac when first platted in 1859. Garrard knew the railroad was due to come through, and in order to prevent the noisy, sooty trains from encroaching on the charming village, he donated land for a railroad station three miles inland, naming it Frontenac Station. Garrard was a smart businessman: not only did he preserve the pastoral landscape of Frontenac for himself, selected residents, and a growing number of tourists drawn to the exclusive resort community, he also took advantage of the economic benefits the railroad offered. Shuttling visitors, residents, and supplies between the station and Frontenac, a stagecoach made its way along what is now a county road that connects to busy Highway 61.

Florence Township Hall, 1974

Township hall stage, with original backdrop

In 1872, Garrard drew up designs for Frontenac Station that included some ten blocks of stores, a church, a post office, a creamery, a train depot, and the town hall. Frontenac Station and Frontenac were and still are part of Florence Township, named in honor of Florence Graham, the daughter of Judge Christopher Graham of Red Wing.

Most town halls in rural areas were hubs for government proceedings and social activities, and the Florence Town Hall was no exception. The building hosted dances, church suppers, and band concerts. The Frontenac Dramatic Club staged productions under the watchful eye of Celestine Schaller, who also owned the Frontenac Inn. Many hotel guests attended the productions, as did townsfolk.

The Florence Town Hall, saved and restored by concerned citizens in the 1990s, remains a vital part of the Frontenac community. Various boards, committees, and community groups hold meetings in the historic hall. Voting still takes place there, as do old-time melodramas, now presented for modern-day audiences. Thankfully, some things never change.

OLD FRONTENAC

The busy, technology-driven modern world seems to have passed Old Frontenac by, and some residents are pleased with this state of affairs. The sleepy little village looks quite as it did at the time of the Civil War. The shuttered windows, two-story porches, verandas, and wrought iron gates show the southern influence of General Israel Garrard, the Kentucky man largely responsible for Old Frontenac.

After discovering the area during a hunting trip with his brother in 1854, Garrard teamed up with a Dutch cabinetmaker, Evert Westervelt, and the duo

Lakeside Hotel, 1905

bought some four thousand acres of land. More than three hundred acres were set aside for the town of Westervelt, which later became Frontenac. Garrard hired several hundred southern craftsmen to build his own little oasis on Lake Pepin. The workers constructed several cottages for Garrard and his brothers, grand homes that face Lake Pepin and are known as the Front Row. Garrard's "cottage"

A private home in Old Frontenac, formerly St. Hubert's Lodge

was actually a hunting lodge dubbed St. Hubert's in honor of the patron saint of hunters.

After the Civil War, General Garrard did a lot of entertaining. The lodge was too small for all his guests, so he renovated a grain warehouse down the bluff and near the lake into the thirty-room Lakeside Hotel. Many of his guests stayed to paint and write, and some were quite well known, including Henry Ward Beecher, a prominent clergyman and abolitionist. (His sister, Harriet Beecher Stowe, wrote the popular book *Uncle Tom's Cabin.*) Actress Marie Dressler paid a visit and, in later years, so did writer F. Scott Fitzgerald. The Garrards were refined people, the general known as a charming and generous southern gent. As did many of the era's wealthy gentlemen, Garrard raised horses. Racehorses. He maintained a twenty-two-horse stable and raced Thoroughbreds on a nearby track. Guests entertained themselves at the races and hunted, fished, and sailed during their stay.

Soon known as "the Newport of the Northwest," Frontenac developed a reputation as a lovely resort destination, drawing wealthy tourists up the river to escape the oppressive southern heat. The pastoral little town even caught the attention of Mark Twain, who wrote about seeing the village in his 1883 novel *Life on the Mississippi:* "Then Frontenac looms upon our vision, delightful resort of jaded summer tourists."

The rambling Lakeside Hotel was sold in 1900 and became the Frontenac Inn, which stayed in business for many years. The Methodist Church bought it and several other buildings in the late 1930s to develop a retreat center, which has since closed. General Garrard died in 1901 from burns he sustained when one of his many dogs knocked over a kerosene lamp. He is buried in a small cemetery near the graceful village he created, a place that inspires visitors to relax and enjoy the elegance of another era.

61 South of Old Frontenac, where the road meets up again with Highway 61, on the right stands a set of old stone walls and a gate. It's easy to miss: trees and brush are slowly enveloping the walls, and the road beyond the padlocked gate is overgrown. These were the gates to Bramble Haw. *Bramble Haw:* it sounds like a mythical kingdom or an English country manor. It was actually a little bit of both.

The road that disappears into the woods once led to a charming two-story New England–style cottage, home to Colonel and Mrs. James Munro. The Munros fell in love with the wild beauty of the Frontenac area and bought nearly two hundred acres of land with dreams of living the rest of their lives on the estate they called Bramble Haw. The home was built in 1925, but four years after the Munros moved in, the colonel died.

Mrs. Munro's sister, Nell Mabey, lived in Minneapolis at the time and worked at the *Minneapolis Tribune.* She had been the women's page editor, the church page editor, the author of advice columns for mothers and the lovelorn. Nell decided to move in with her widowed sister, and Bramble Haw is where the former newspaper editor began her second career as a poet.

Miss Mabey, as she was called, claimed that words and phrases for her poems popped into her mind as she worked in the gardens or wandered the woods of Bramble Haw with her beloved dog, Whimpie. The Irish Water Spaniel was the star of Mabey's 1955 book, *Whimpie of Bramble Haw.* Her first collection of poetry, *Clover Blooms,* came out in 1938. As Mabey's poems appeared in a number of national and regional publications, she became one of Minnesota's better-known women poets.

Locked gates to the former site of Bramble Haw

When her sister died in 1953, Nell moved into Lake City. Honoring one of the Munros' final wishes—that their beloved estate be preserved—Nell and others oversaw the creation of Frontenac State Park on the two hundred acres of Bramble Haw. The Munro/Mabey home served as the state park manager's residence and an office for a time before being razed in the 1990s.

The beauty of Bramble Haw and Frontenac was reflected in Nell Mabey's work. Even though the estate is long

OLD FRONTENAC *by Nell Mabey*

A painting done in tender notes
Of mauve and dove, pastels
Of petal shades:
As though from golden songbird
    throats
A carillon of bells
Had shaken apple blossoms down,
Confettilike . . . sweet peas
In cool cascades . . .
All about the little town
Are flower pots at ease.

At Frontenac, bewitched
    with joy,
The clocks are motionless;
The old ones say
Some Joshua-minded, princely boy,
To keep his happiness,
Hold fast his moment's ecstasy,
Commanded them to cease . . .
And to this day
They stand at High Felicity
Against the chimney piece.

gone, the dreams that inspired it remain. From the dust cover of Nell's last book, one sentence evokes the memory of this special place: "Bramble Haw lives forever, seen as in a glass, and not darkly, but in dancing, prismatic lights."

LAKE CITY CLAMMING

One of the last vestiges of the Lake Pepin clamming industry is on the corner of Washington and Marion streets, a block off Highway 61 in the business district of Lake City. It's easy to miss the sign for the Lake Pepin Pearl Button Company because the letters, high up on the two-story, cream brick building, are very faint. The building was actually used as a button-making business for only a short time. In the mid-1870s, it was Finch's Dry Goods Store; later it was a shirt-making factory. The button business moved in from 1915 to 1919. A casket company took over in the early 1920s, but throughout the years the Lake Pepin Pearl Button Company name has remained. The buttons produced here weren't made of pearls, however. Their pearl-like, iridescent sheen came from clamshells dredged from nearby Lake Pepin in a process known as clamming.

Clamming—harvesting freshwater mussels for their shells and pearls—started around Clinton, Iowa, in 1880 and pushed its way up the Mississippi River. The first button factory was built in Muscatine, Iowa, in 1890, and demand became so great that as many as twenty-five hundred people were employed in button-related businesses, making Muscatine the "Pearl Button Capital of the World." As the lus-

trous clamshell buttons grew in popularity, clamming became a big industry for the little towns along Lake Pepin and the Mississippi from Lake City down to Wabasha, Minnesota, and on the Wisconsin side from Pepin to Alma.

Clamming was done mostly during the summer months. Rosa Larson of Pepin remembers clamming with her parents and three other families in the Deer Island area of Lake Pepin, where they'd pitch canvas over wooden boards to make a tent cabin and stay on the river

Lake Pepin Pearl Button Company

until school started. It was one of the happiest times of Rosa's life as she played with the other children while her parents worked the clam beds.

It wasn't an easy job. Clammers used low-slung, flat-bottomed boats that were usually square at each end. The boats had several nine-foot-long bars with claw-foot hooks that fastened to a couple of upright poles. To start the clamming operation, the boat was rowed away from its anchor and the bars dropped into the water and dragged across the river bottom. When the hook touched a partially opened clam, the mussel snapped shut and held on tight. When the clammer drifted over a particularly well-populated clam bed, the hooks could fill up in fewer than fifteen minutes.

The boats were about five feet wide to handle the load of clams tossed in the bottom. One Lake City clammer, Ed Storing, in an oral history for the Wabasha County Historical Society, remembered that his boat could be so thick with clams that it would be tough to remain upright while walking around the boat to operate the bars and winches. The slimy clams' odor probably wasn't all that appetizing on the boat, but onshore the stench was even stronger. The clams were dumped into a large cooker and steamed open. After about fifteen minutes, the clammer— or, often, the clammer's wife—dug out the meat, carefully feeling around for the elusive pearl. At this stage of the process, clammers were like gold prospectors, always hoping to discover something of impressive value. Lake Pepin clams usually produced the largest pearls, which were quite popular in Paris and London.

THE JEWELL NURSERY, ESTABLISHED IN 1868 AND IN BUSINESS THROUGH THE TWENTIETH CENTURY, WAS A FAR-FLUNG OPERATION COVERING SOME FIFTEEN HUNDRED ACRES OUTSIDE OF LAKE CITY AND EMPLOYING TWO HUNDRED WORKERS. IN 2000, THE LAND WAS PURCHASED FOR A GOLF COURSE AND HOUSING DEVELOPMENT.

The "pearl man," or buyer, came around a few times during the summer as Rosa Larson's family clammed off Deer Island. When he left, she said, "then we'd have money!" Buyers were willing to pay good prices for any pearl that matched in color, size, and shape the specimens they already had. Ed Storing remembered hearing of one Lake Pepin pearl that fetched more than a thousand dollars. The April 1909 edition of the *American Thresherman* reported, "A pearl buyer finds his work most fascinating; not every merchant can take his entire stock out of his vest pocket, lay it on the table and sort it in little piles the size of a nickel." Other pearl buyers were a little more cautious with their treasures, carrying them in cases lined with oiled silk.

Clammers also made money from selling tons of clamshells to the button-making companies. Clams with fanciful names like "Lady Finger," "Elephant Ear," "Monkey Face," and "Glass Back" were among the many species plucked from the bottom of the river. The most sought-after clam was the "Ebony Shell," whose thick casing was perfect for button making. Prices varied, ranging from seven to fifteen to sixty-five dollars a ton, depending on the economy and on availability.

A fisherman's camp, clamshells piled high, ca. 1900

Piles of clamshells were sent to a Wabasha button factory as well as to the Lake Pepin Pearl Button Company and other workshops in Lake City. "Blanks" were carefully sawed out of the shell, holes added for thread, and the buttons smoothed and polished to a glossy sheen, tacked onto cards, and sent off to stores. The leftover clamshell, several holes drilled out of it, was ground up and distributed to poultry farmers.

By the 1920s, it became harder to find the right kinds of clams for button making. When clamming was at its height, thirty-two species could be found from Red Wing to Wabasha, in clam beds that were often a mile long and three feet deep. In 1914, an estimated three to four thousand tons of clams were taken from Lake Pepin and about one hundred clamming boats plied its waters. In the following years, these figures started to drop. Many of the clam beds were nearly picked clean, and some species were so overfished that they became threatened or extinct.

Lake Pepin was closed to clamming from 1919 until 1924 to allow the clam beds to regenerate. By that time, however, the clamming industry was getting hit on another front as Japan began exporting cheaper buttons to the United States. According to clammers like Ed Storing, it seemed that all at once the button and clam businesses bottomed out. By the mid-1930s, clamming had all but stopped at Reads Landing, downstream from Lake City. And in the end, there was no need for clamshell buttons when plastic ones would do.

Ongoing efforts seek to save Lake Pepin's native clams, now reeling from the effects of pollution and damage caused by invasive species like zebra mussels. Clams have played an important role in the river's ecology and history, and their beautiful, opalescent shells and the occasional gift of a nearly perfect pearl are lovely reminders as to why they need to be protected always.

Clamshells and buttons

READS LANDING

61 Looking around Reads Landing today, it is hard to believe that this sleepy little village was once a rollicking river town and a potential site for the Minnesota state capitol. Situated at the confluence of the Chippewa and Mississippi rivers, it was a natural spot for business and transportation. Logs cut by Wisconsin lumberjacks floated down the Chippewa, and here as many as three hundred workers gathered them into rafts and guided the loads of lumber down the Mississippi. Sometimes the floating logs took up more than three acres of the river. As many as two thousand log rafts left Reads Landing each year until 1915, when many of the choicest trees had been cut and logging in Wisconsin started to wane.

The area had been a favorite gathering place for local Native Americans, who called it *Waumadee*. The Dakota trading post was eventually purchased by Charles Read. Because of its location, Reads Landing became a convenient steamboat stop. A ferry service connected Reads Landing and Nelson, Wisconsin, just across the river. Twenty-seven hotels were built to meet the needs of passengers coming and going; for those seeking some entertainment, there were almost as many saloons. Reads Landing developed a raucous reputation, and many stories tell of the fights and other high jinks that occurred, especially when the lumberjacks and raftsmen were in town. The Bullard House, built in 1859, was known as the best hotel on the river.

It wasn't unusual for as many as thirty steamboats to hold up at Reads Landing

Reads Landing, 1885

The Reads Landing school is now home to the Wabasha County Historical Society.

in the early spring, waiting for the ice on Lake Pepin to break up before traveling farther north. The passengers and riverboat crews, sometimes numbering as many as fifteen hundred, made the village look like a thriving city. Reads Landing also became one of the country's busiest wheat shipping ports for a time, its levee clogged with farmers bargaining for a good price on their grain.

Flush with cash, the town spent more than eight thousand dollars on a new school in 1870. The two-story Italianate building was only the second such brick school in Minnesota. But life in Reads Landing began to change the next year when the Chicago, Milwaukee and St. Paul Railroad came through. The railroad ultimately sapped much of the town's importance as a shipping center. Business prospects started to melt away, and with them, people.

Only a couple of old brick buildings

remain on what was the landing by the river. The stately brick schoolhouse still holds its lofty position on the hillside. It is now home to the Wabasha County Historical Society and a treasure trove of artifacts from a time when Reads Landing shared the stage with some of Minnesota's most important cities.

WABASHA COUNTY POOR HOUSE

61 When the modern, four-lane version of Highway 61 was built in the 1970s, a portion of the road's original alignment became Wabasha County Road 30. Even to early motorists, the cluster of old brick buildings surrounded by farm fields may have looked out of place. They certainly do today. Here stand the Wabasha County Poor House's original structures, stark reminders of how society once dealt with its poorest and most vulnerable.

Being poor was considered disgraceful. A popular (and misguided) belief put forth that the poor were that way because of slovenly habits or some kind of character defect. Prior to the establishment of poorhouses, communities dealt with the indigent in several ways.

If an individual or family fell on hard times and relatives or a church organization couldn't provide enough help, a locally elected overseer of the poor used public money to provide these less fortunate souls with food and clothing. Sometimes a community contracted with local residents, paying them to provide care for a group of paupers—the small-town version of a county poorhouse. Finally, believe it or not, some communities put up the poor for auction. This practice amounted to slavery, as the pauper or an entire family was sold to the lowest bidder, who promised to provide housing, food, clothing, and health care in exchange for free labor. As the United States grew, so did concerns about dealing with the nation's poor. By the mid- to late 1800s, taxpayer-supported, county-run poorhouses were popping up around the country. In 1864, the Minnesota legislature mandated that every county was responsible for the care of its destitute citizens.

WABASHA IS KNOWN FOR GOOD BASS FISHING THANKS TO ITS LOCATION NEAR LAKE PEPIN AND THE MISSISSIPPI'S BACKWATERS, WHICH ARE PRIME BASS HIDING PLACES. SEVERAL BIG FISHING TOURNAMENTS ARE HELD IN THE AREA EVERY YEAR.

The Wabasha County Poor House was one of sixty-four such facilities built in Minnesota between 1854 and 1926. One of the first buildings on the thirty-two-acre site was a two-story brick hospital, built in 1879. A larger, thirty-room dormitory was built next door in 1883, housing the superintendent's quarters, a kitchen, a dining room, and resident bedrooms. At the time it opened, residents numbered "seventeen persons, among them three insane, one idiotic and one blind." People who lost their jobs or their minds or both were likely to end up at the poorhouse, as were the destitute elderly, the physically disabled, and orphaned children. While the initial motivation behind the poorhouse system may have been good, many residents eventually found themselves in deplorable conditions.

State investigators assessed facilities in need of repair. Many were simply big old farmhouses that were falling apart, tough to heat, and difficult to keep clean and vermin free. At the Wabasha County Poor House, inspectors found the second-story floors had "large cracks and could not be scrubbed well because the boards were so leaky." Many county poorhouses became overcrowded. Ill and contagious residents often were not quarantined. Some sitting rooms and dining rooms became bedrooms. At the nearby Winona County institution, an inspector was dismayed to find unrelated men and women living in the same rooms. The inspector warned, "Scandals have occurred in the past and are liable to occur again." In some cases, residents were abused physically. Many babies were born out of wedlock in these institutions.

Wabasha County Poor House, 1890

Despite these appalling conditions, a 1925 nationwide report found that many of Minnesota's poorhouses were actually better than average, with residents receiving compassionate if not entirely adequate care. The Wabasha County Poor House operated under county supervision until the 1930s. At that time, many residents were required to leave in order to qualify for old-age assistance payments or pensions. The county board decided to lease the facility to a private operator, making it a for-profit rest home and allowing residents to stay but still collect their pensions.

The former poorhouse buildings haven't changed much.

The Jo Ann Rest Home remained open until 1952. It sat empty for several years until a local man purchased it, moved his chicken farm to the site, and in the 1970s operated the Velvet Rooster restaurant out of the old dormitory building. The owner had plans to develop the acres of farmland around the old poorhouse but soon found that more than eighty Indian burial mounds were sprinkled over the acreage. He also discovered an unmarked cemetery where some of the poorhouse residents are buried. Sadly, those who wound up in poorhouses often were not only hidden from society but also died unknown, faceless and nameless.

The Wabasha County Poor House is one of the state's last, most intact examples of how the poor and elderly lived their lives before the advent of modern-day assistance programs and Social Security. It was included in the National Register of Historic Places in 1982. Coming almost full circle, the old thirty-room dormitory and adjoining hospital are now home to a number of residents from the Wabasha area.

ROLLINGSTONE COLONY

61 The tragic tale of the Rollingstone Colony merits a small sign just off Highway 61 in Minnesota City. Most drivers motor past, not bothering to stop and read it. It's their loss, however, because there are few tales like it in Minnesota history.

The story began in New York City in the summer of 1851. Printer William Haddock held meetings and promoted the idea of leaving the filthy, overcrowded city and heading west to start a new life on free government land. The plan was to develop a self-sustaining community, a well-planned city with a hospital, a courthouse, and a university. Membership was limited to five hundred people. Even women could become landowners under Haddock's proposal. He launched the Western Farm and Village Association and drummed up interest through his publication,

Certificate granted to investors in William Haddock's dream

the *Western Farm and Village Advocate*. Hundreds joined: clergymen, doctors, mechanics, tradespeople, lawyers—all bought into William Haddock's Rollingstone City. Even the *New York Tribune* endorsed the venture.

The idea of forming self-sustaining communal colonies had been tried before. New Harmony in Indiana dissolved in 1828. Another utopian experiment, Brook Farm in Roxbury, Massachusetts, formed in 1841 but disbanded in 1847. Haddock's dream would fade away even faster.

Haddock and another man set out to find land on which to build Rollingstone City, heading for Minnesota Territory in the winter of 1852. As early as the 1840s, Minnesota had been advertised as a beautiful place with fresh water and abundant land. From Chicago, Haddock wrote to the association members: "We have ridden every day, except one, and slept only every other night." On a Mississippi steamboat they ran into ice at La Crosse; undaunted, they strapped on ice skates and continued up the river. They passed present-day Winona, and a few miles upriver they found the perfect place for their new city. Or so they thought.

Haddock's partner returned to New York with a rough plat of the area and quickly drew up a lithographed map. Upon their arrival, the soon-to-be-settlers were to draw lots for a home in the village and more than 150 acres of land in the valley.

Early in the spring of 1852, steamboat captains at Galena, Illinois, were met by a group of excited easterners who said they were bound for Rollingstone City, north of La Crosse. Knowing every inch of the river, the skeptical captains told them they were crazy: there was no such town. To the captains' surprise, the visitors had beautifully detailed maps that clearly showed a large city with blocks of neatly laid-out homes, parks, and a glass-enclosed greenhouse to grow vegetables in the winter. The puzzled captains figured the site had to be several miles beyond Wapasha's Prairie (now Winona). They dropped off the settlers and all their belongings as instructed, but Haddock had made a terrible mistake. The land he claimed while under the winter's deep snow was actually a swampy slough about a mile from the Mississippi, full of snakes and chilly, muddy water.

One of the befuddled settlers, Reverend Edward Ely, wrote in a May 10, 1852, diary entry: "The water is four feet deep in the slough, and is still rising. There are no teams [of horses] to be had. There is no road for the next six miles and no bridge."

With no way to send word back east, waves of Western Farm and Village Association members kept coming. By the end of May, approximately four hundred people were "settled" in what turned out to be nothing more than a city on paper. Most were women and children. All were completely unprepared for the difficult conditions. The woman and children slept in a large tent; the men in log-sided "gopher pits" covered with grass. Measles and cholera swept through the colony, killing almost three-quarters of the settlers. At the first opportunity, the survivors either returned east or migrated to Winona. Some stayed and began the town known as Minnesota City—one of the oldest in the state.

All that remains of William Haddock's doomed venture are some weathered graves, faded diary entries, and the ruins of an old mill. And the small roadside marker, which ends with a huge understatement: "the colony gradually declined."

THE OAKS

61 Just down from the Rollingstone Colony marker, a boxy gray warehouse sits by itself across from Garvin Creek. Today the roof of the nondescript building is barely visible from the highway. But there was a time when motorists on Highway 61, which once passed through Minnesota City, couldn't have missed the building's big sign or the packed parking lot. Here was the Oaks Supper Club, one of the hottest restaurants and nightclubs between the Twin Cities and Chicago.

SLOT MACHINES WERE AT THE OAKS AND OTHER ESTABLISHMENTS ACROSS THE STATE IN THE 1930S AND EARLY 1940S UNTIL THEY WERE BANNED UNDER A LAW SIGNED BY GOVERNOR LUTHER YOUNGDAHL IN 1946.

THE OAKS NITE CLUB
The Finest in The Northwest
Winona, Minn.

THE OAKS NITE CLUB

8717

The Oaks, 1950s

The original building was a brewery built in 1864 by Otto Vill, whose brew earned a gold medal at the Paris Exposition. The Vills turned the brewery into a hotel and saloon in 1918, calling it the Grove Hotel in honor of the nearby oak trees. The little oak grove started to attract a lot of attention in 1930 when the Oaks Nite Club opened. In the basement: high stakes gambling, with slot machines, poker tables, and a roulette wheel. Upstairs: dancing and dining. But there was one prob-

*Memorabilia of the
Oaks Nite Club*

lem—the food. Seeking a tasty solution, the owners lured chef Walt Kelly from Minneapolis.

Kelly was not only a master chef; he was a consummate host and a world-class promoter. An ample man with a kind face and small mustache, he was regularly spotted welcoming diners and going table to table in his white chef's smock and sky-high chef's hat. Kelly remembered the trepidation the club's owners felt when he suggested offering an all-you-can-eat smorgasbord of beef, roast pork, turkey, ham, lobster, scallops, fish, baked oysters, vegetables, salads, and fancy desserts for seventy-five cents. Who would show up for such an expensive buffet? The first week, three hundred curious diners came; the following week, seven hundred. Every Thursday, the buffet drew hundreds, as many as 875 one night.

As the Oaks' reputation grew, so did the guest list. The sixty staff members were known for their hospitality. Many diners were shocked when the head waitress welcomed them by name. Her secret: a three-ring binder with a customer list of some twelve thousand names that she checked before guests arrived.

Some of the patrons, drawn to the downstairs gambling, were said to have shady reputations. Gangsters of any importance traveled in and out of St. Paul and Minneapolis in the 1930s. Alvin "Creepy" Karpis called St. Paul a "crooks' haven." John Dillinger got into a gun battle with police in St. Paul and escaped an ambush in Hastings. "Baby Face" Nelson robbed the Brainerd bank. Gangsters and bootleggers worked throughout the region in the 1930s, and, not surprisingly, the popular Oaks was associated with gangster tales. Once, federal agents were tipped that Al Capone was going to show up, but to the best of anyone's memory he stayed away. Stories of secret underground passageways that were escape routes to Garvin Creek for gangsters and gamblers trying to elude police—according to Kelly's son, Walt—were simply that: stories. Passageways do exist under the building, but the narrow halls were for storing beer barrels during its days as a brewery.

The Oaks suffered a major blow in 1946 when a fire destroyed much of the building. As Chef Kelly set about rebuilding, he had a couple of goals in mind: the place was going to be his dream nightclub, and it wasn't going to burn down again. Kelly toured nightclubs in Chicago, St. Louis, and the Twin Cities to get ideas for the perfect place. He also made sure the building was fireproof, with fire walls and flame-retardant concrete from the ceiling to the floors.

The New Oaks, bigger and better, sleek and smart looking, opened in 1948 to rave reviews: the Winona paper called it "as modern as tomorrow." The huge dining room sat six hundred, and the stage was large enough to hold a sixteen-piece orchestra. The eighty-seven-foot bar was dubbed "the longest West of the Mississippi." Ten bartenders kept the cocktails flowing. Las Vegas–style floor shows packed people in. Walt Kelly remembers ice being manufactured for one show that had skaters performing to music. The parade of celebrities and entertainers kept coming as the Oaks became a major stop between Chicago and the Twin Cities. Big-name, big band acts like Lawrence Welk and Sammy Kaye played the Oaks. The

Three Stooges entertained young Walt Kelly and other guests with their slapstick antics. The Oaks and a smaller club across the creek, the Acorn, put Minnesota City on the entertainment map.

Chef Kelly died in 1957, but by then the club's popularity was already beginning to slip. His son, Walt, lists several reasons for the decline. Among them was the advent of television, which ate into the Oaks' business by keeping people home instead of bringing them out to dine, dance, and drink as they had in the

This building once housed the Oaks.

past. Mrs. Kelly tried to maintain the club amid many challenges, but she finally sold the property. The Oaks has been the site of several other businesses, ranging from a dinner theater to a church to its present incarnation as a machine shop.

The Oaks may be gone, but countless memories are forever stored within the building's cinder block walls. It takes a little imagination, but the parking lot, packed with Studebakers, Packards, and Hudsons, comes to life and in the trees one can almost hear the swinging band music and Chef Kelly's laugh as he welcomed his many guests.

SUGAR LOAF

61 One of the most photographed landmarks in Winona is Sugar Loaf, a rocky pinnacle perched on a limestone bluff overlooking the junction of Highways 61 and 43. Some may wonder how Mother Nature managed to create such an unusual rock formation. The truth is that she didn't: workmen did.

The bluff used to have a rounded dome topped with a crown of evergreens. The landmark was well known to early explorers and the native Indians. The 1938 WPA

Guide to Minnesota gives a fanciful description of how the Mdewakanton Sioux gathered at the base of the bluff for ceremonies of "barbaric splendor." The Indians called the top Wa-pah-sha's Cap because it looked like the headpiece worn by Chief Wapasha (or Wabasha).

Two brothers began quarrying operations on Wa-pah-sha's Cap after a huge 1862 fire destroyed much of downtown Winona, including the wood plank sidewalks. Blasting operations chiseled away most of the bluff top; the limestone was

Sugar Loaf reflected in Lake Winona

THE REMAINS OF A BREWERY THAT MADE BUB'S BEER STAND AT THE BASE OF SUGAR LOAF. THE BREWERY CLOSED IN 1969.

used for Winona's new sidewalks and buildings. The quarry was shut down in 1887, and what remains is Sugar Loaf, so named for its resemblance to sugar packages of times past.

Sugar Loaf has lost a little heft over the years: in 2004, tons of eroded limestone broke away and cascaded down the face of the bluff, stopping just short of a house. Sugar Loaf aside, Winona is blessed with gorgeous geology. Picturesque bluffs rise up alongside the river, which is fed by streams that have cut deep into the limestone to make rocky coulees. The Winona area is part of what geologists call the driftless area for its lack of glacial drift, the material left behind by melting glaciers. This region includes southeastern Minnesota, northeastern Iowa, southwestern Wisconsin, and parts of northwestern Illinois. Mother Nature's handiwork or not, the views along this stretch of Highway 61 are breathtaking.

61 Remember door-to-door salesmen who'd hawk everything from encyclopedias to vacuum cleaners? Some were known simply by the stuff they sold, identified as the "Fuller Brush Man" or the "Watkins Man." The Watkins Man was one of an army of traveling salesmen for the Winona-based J. R. Watkins Company.

The company headquarters and plant are a Winona landmark, although Mr. Watkins began his business in Plainview, Minnesota. Joseph Ray Watkins experimented with various ingredients in his kitchen, creating a potent liniment that could be used on horses and humans. He bottled the potion in his woodshed and in 1868 started selling it to local farmers, traveling from farm to farm in his horse and buggy. Watkins made a name for himself and his Red Liniment based in part on a clever strategy: he guaranteed customer satisfaction or a full refund.

Watkins's business outgrew his woodshed, and in 1885 he moved to the bustling lumber and milling town of Winona. This important Mississippi River port was served by no fewer than five railroads, making it the perfect place for an entrepreneur like Watkins. He changed the firm's name to the J. R. Watkins Medical Company and added items like Petro-Carbo Salve and Carthartic Pills, plus a full line of spices and extracts.

Mr. Brown, the traveling Watkins Man, ca. 1900

Watkins hired salesmen to fan out across the region and eventually the nation, bringing products directly to customers. The company and its offerings became quite popular in rural areas, and a visit from the Watkins Man was a major event. Many people remember how the Watkins salesman's "rolling store" smelled of vanilla and spices with just a whiff of liniment and salve. He may have had a trinket or piece of candy for the kids, and he always brought local news along with his wares. The Watkins Man stopped by every two or three months, saving rural customers a long trip into town.

Watkins soon found he needed help managing his multimillion-dollar enterprise and convinced his nephew, Paul, to move to Winona and become the firm's vice president. Watkins opened branches across the country during the 1890s and its first international office in Canada in 1913. Riding a wave of success and profits, Watkins hired noted Prairie school architect George Washington Maher to build a new headquarters for the firm. J. R. Watkins didn't live to see Maher's magnificent $1.2 million building, resplendent with Italian tile and marble and a breathtaking Louis Millet–designed stained-glass window over the front doors of the foyer. He died in 1911.

Watkins Building, 1945

By the 1940s, Watkins products were being sold across the United States, Canada, Australia, South Africa, and England, making it one of the world's largest direct-sales companies. But things started changing—and quickly—for Watkins after World War II. Loyal rural customers were more mobile, and many left the farm for the city. The venerable company couldn't keep up with shifting demographics and buying habits, and it filed for bankruptcy in the 1970s. Minneapolis financier Irwin Jacobs purchased it in 1978.

There are still tens of thousands of Watkins independent salespeople, but now nationwide stores like Wal-Mart and Target carry certain Watkins items and the company sells its products online. Still, the glorious Watkins Building in Winona stands in testimony to an earlier time, when the Watkins Man might come knocking on the farmhouse door.

61 Early highway construction was destructive and often altered the character of a place forever. One path was determined to be the most efficient route, and whatever was in the way of the soon-to-be road was moved or bulldozed. What was once known as the Minne-O-Wah Club is a case in point.

A summer colony nestled amid the river bluffs a few miles out of town, the club was founded by a dozen well-off and well-known men from Winona in 1902. About fifty years before the colony was created, Minneowah had been a small town, at least for a short time.

Willard Bunnell gave Minneowah its name in 1853, using an Indian word for "falling water" or "snow water" because of the icy springs that bubbled out of the rocks there. Several stockholders, all prominent men of "considerable capital," wanted to develop a city that would rival Winona in prominence. In the spring of 1853, a large hotel, a few stores, and a handful of dwellings were built at a location just above the village of Homer. Upper Minneowah was to be made up of five- to ten-acre suburban lots for homes. During the hot summer months, the wealthy St. Paul–based businessmen visited their investment property to cool off and enjoy the refreshing spring water. But by the fall, things started going wrong. One of the original investors in the scheme died; another sold his holdings. An official with the Minneowah Stock Company had evidently forgotten to secure a title to the site, and the town plot was never recorded. Some of those living in Minneowah decided to file claims with the U.S. Land Office declaring themselves as settlers. They were awarded homesteads, and Minneowah was divided up. Daniel Dougherty drew the hotel and a store and a sizable chunk of land. That rankled Willard Bunnell, who fought Mr. Dougherty over the matter. The fight ended when Dougherty nearly bit off Bunnell's thumb.

Minne-O-Wah Club, 1914

There was no such nastiness decades later when the gentlemen of the Minne-O-Wah Club purchased the land in order to build summer cottages to escape the hot and humid city of Winona. It was a well-planned communal vacation spot, with a central kitchen and dining hall, a head cook and several maids, a clubhouse, swimming pool, and tennis courts. Lots were leased to members, but each man owned his own cottage, one of eleven on the site. Each family had its own table in the dining area, and each wife decorated as she chose with her own place mats, tablecloth, napkins, and centerpieces. Groceries were delivered from Winona by horse and wagon and later by truck once or twice a week. Those who spent their summers at the Minne-O-Wah Club recall the simple but delicious food: Sunday dinners of fried chicken with homemade ice cream; green apple pies, applesauce, and cherry pies made from fruit trees on the grounds. Residents were summoned to meals by a clanging bell. And after dinner on Sunday nights, everyone gathered around the clubhouse piano to sing hymns.

Club members enjoyed this idyllic existence. Husbands commuted into Winona daily for work while wives stayed at the colony with the children. Laundry was sent to town. All that remained was to read, chat, do some needlework, and watch

A remaining Minne-O-Wah cottage, likely dating to 1930

after the children. Those youngsters remember glorious summers, the bluffs and the nearby river serving as their playground.

What caused Minne-O-Wah's downfall isn't exactly clear. At least one longtime member resigned in 1933. One member died. According to the *Winona Saturday Morning Post,* the club didn't open in the summer of 1942, although some remaining club members did use their cottages. The clubhouse was sold to a private buyer, along with the swimming pool and the caretaker's cottage.

Some of the cottages were moved up the bluff when Highway 61 came through; others were destroyed. Bits of the old Minne-O-Wah—including at least two intact cottages—remain, visible only to the informed eye. Despite some remodeling, one of them, high on the bluff, still retains the feel of a cozy summer getaway, with echoes of a more genteel time.

EMIL AND THE OTTERS

"See the Otters" signs were posted for years on Highway 61 in the Homer area. They pointed tourists to Emil Liers Trained Otter Farm and what the 1946 AAA tour guide described as "the only trained otters in the United States." Admission, by the way, was twenty cents for adults, a dime for kids. Who could pass up a chance to see otters, and trained ones at that?

left: Emil Liers at his otter sanctuary, 1960s

above: Emil Liers and friend, 1960s

Emil Liers himself was an interesting guy. Born in Clayton, Iowa, Liers moved to the Winona area and was a trapper in the 1920s. His career and life changed one day as he was removing a dead otter from one of his traps. He heard the plaintive yipping of two otter pups, clearly pining for their mother. Feeling bad, Emil scooped up the babies and brought them home. He never set another trap. The otters thrived under Emil's care. Up to that point, no one had successfully raised otters in a domesticated environment. Then Emil's otters reproduced in captivity, another first. Emil became an otter expert and opened a sanctuary near Homer. But it wasn't the typical roadside zoo and tourist trap: it had a greater purpose.

Otters, cute as they are, were considered vermin by fishermen. Thinking the otters ate too many fish, anglers made a point of shooting or trapping them. Dogs were specially trained to hunt and kill otters. By the 1930s, the otter population had dropped dramatically. But Emil Liers discovered that his otters actually liked crawfish and frogs better than fish. He traveled the country with the critters, educating people about these intelligent and affectionate animals. Experts now credit Liers for helping to save this once endangered species. Liers and his work were the subject of many articles in magazines like *National Geographic, Life, Time,* and *Newsweek.*

Emil also drew attention for successfully training his otters to act like any good hunting dog would. They could follow a scent, retrieve ducks and pheasants, and entertain with a few good tricks. Liers's otters clearly had an affinity for him. Photographs show Emil walking through the snow and looking like the Pied Piper with several otters scampering behind. Liers wrote a number of nature books for children, including the 1952 *An Otter's Story* that led to the Walt Disney movie *Flash: The Teenaged Otter*. His otters found roles in this and other movies, and Emil served as a technical consultant on the films. Many Minnesotans had the chance to see Emil's otters in person. Busloads of schoolchildren stopped by every year; in the 1950s, as many as ten thousand people visited the Homer otter sanctuary.

Liers died in 1975 at the age of eighty-five, decades after his life took an interesting turn when he became a surrogate father to a pair of orphaned otters.

LA CRESCENT APPLES

61 Near the Minnesota-Wisconsin border is the town of La Crescent. Its romantic name is attributed to the Kentucky Land Company's marketing of the area. Speculators and developers arrived in what was known as Manton in 1856. The Kentucky Land Company built a dozen homes to sell to settlers but reasoned that a more idyllic-sounding name would better attract buyers. The town is on a bend of the Mississippi River that looks somewhat like a crescent and, if the story is to be believed, for this reason the dignified name of La Crescent was chosen.

La Crescent is called the Apple Capitol of Minnesota, and for good reason. The

Leidel's Orchard, in business since 1917

area might not have as many orchards as it once did, but it was the first place in the state to successfully grow apples. Early settlers had tried and failed to cultivate apple trees in the harsh climate, but that was before the arrival of John Samuel Harris.

Harris was an Ohio native who grew up loving all manner of plants and trees. He arrived in Minnesota in 1856, one year before the town of La Crescent was incorporated. He and his wife and two children started Sunny Side Garden and grew vegetables and berries. Harris, intrigued by the assumption that apple trees simply could not be grown in Minnesota, began experimenting. Each year, he planted as many species of apple trees and other fruit trees as he could get his hands on. People were skeptical, and Harris probably had his own doubts when the brutal winters of 1872–73 and 1884–85 nearly wiped out all his trees.

Governor Youngdahl promoting Minnesota apples, 1949

But Harris was not one to give up. He wondered whether, just as people need to acclimate, the delicate trees would need to grow accustomed to the climate in order to thrive. He bet that while the first and second generations of trees might fall victim to the cold, the third and fourth and subsequent generations would be tough enough to take it.

Harris planted trees and took seeds from their apples and planted them. When the trees from those seeds bore apples, he continued the cycle until he finally grew trees that seemed to withstand the Minnesota climate. Harris also credited the Houston County soil for his horticultural success, writing that it was the best in the state for raising fruit trees because of a proper mix of clay and sandy loam. John Harris became a founding member of the Minnesota State Horticultural Society after shocking state fairgoers in Rochester in 1866 with the largest display of home-grown fruit ever seen to that point in Minnesota. By 1895, orchards appeared in several other Minnesota towns and as far north as Duluth.

La Crescent remained an apple-growing mecca long after Harris's death in 1901. By the 1940s, almost forty small orchards were in business in and around La Crescent. There are fewer apple orchards today, but tourists still make the drive down Highway 61 to buy the fruit made famous through the efforts of John Harris, "Father of the Orchardists."

APPLEFEST, HELD THE THIRD WEEKEND IN SEPTEMBER, BEGAN IN 1949 AS A WAY TO PUT LA CRESCENT'S APPLE INDUSTRY IN THE PUBLIC EYE.

Epilogue

Far too often nowadays, we pack up the car or SUV, strap the kids in the back, pop in a DVD to keep them quiet, and then drive—fast—from Point A to Point B in an effort to arrive at our destination as quickly as possible. That is a shame. A wise man, Dave Nystuen, who used to work at the Minnesota Historical Society as a roadside history expert, once told me that in order to see history, one has to get off the freeway and out of the car. History surrounds us: we just have to open our eyes and look for it. Most of us are too busy to do so. Early highway travelers viewed a road trip as something to look forward to, a grand adventure. I hope you'll take the time to meander along Highway 61 and other routes throughout Minnesota. Support local efforts to preserve history: it adds a little meaning and color to life's journey.

I'll see you down the road. Safe travels!

Acknowledgments

A project like this one has a lot of similarities to a long road trip. Despite having a map, sometimes you get lost, or there's a vehicle breakdown, or the car runs out of gas. This journey was certainly an adventure, and the following people made wonderful traveling companions.

Special thanks to Mom, Dad, and Eric for their unwavering support; Denny Behr for his patience, perseverance, and phenomenal photographic skills; Brendan Henehan and Martha Sawyer Allen for their wise words and sharp eyes; Sandy DiNanni and Linda James for top-notch research assistance; and Shannon Pennefeather for taking my words and making them so much better.

Thanks also to Walt Bennick, Winona County Historical Society; John Bray, MnDOT/Duluth District; Sean Dowse, Sheldon Theatre, Red Wing; Anne Dugan, Carlton County Historical Society; Glenn Griffin, HBI Inc.; Char Henn, Goodhue County Historical Society; Walt Kelly, Winona; Skip and Linda Lamb, Schroeder; Patricia Maus, Northeast Minnesota Historical Center, University of Minnesota at Duluth; Alta McQuatters, Lutsen; Alvera Pierson and Alvin Anderson, Duluth; Lee Radzak, Split Rock Lighthouse; Paul Sundberg, Gooseberry Falls State Park; Rick Tokarczyk, Lake County Historical Society; Steve Trimble, St. Paul; Bernie Young, Silver Bay; and Pat Zankman, Cook County Historical Society.

Notes

HIGHWAY 61—THE ROAD

S. Rex Green, "A History of the North Shore Road" (paper delivered to the North Shore Historical Assembly, Duluth, MN, October 17, 1940), S. Rex Green Papers, Minnesota Historical Society, 1.

Barbara Henning, "Phase II Investigation: Trunk Highway 61—Duluth to Canadian Border," Report to the Minnesota Department of Transportation (Santa Fe, NM: Rivercrest Associates, 2004), 2–7.

Minnesota Department of Highways, "History and Organization of the Department of Highways: State of Minnesota," conducted in cooperation with the Public Roads Administration of the Federal Works Agency (March 1942), 7–8, 11–12.

Andrew Munsch, "Lost Minnesota Highways," www.deadpioneer.com.

"The New Lake Superior International Highway" pamphlet, 1933, 13, author's collection.

"North Shore Road Is Being Marked. Duluth–Port Arthur Road Made Part of the Black and White System," *Cook County News Herald,* July 11, 1917.

Thomas Roeser, *Ingenious Deceit: The Real Story of Highway 35, the Scandal that Never Existed* (St. Paul, MN: self-published, 1964).

"Scores Herald Opening of International Highway," *Duluth Herald,* July 11, 1925, quoting Charles Babcock.

OUTLAW BRIDGE

"Bridge Over Pigeon River Now a Reality," *Cook County News Herald,* May 2, 1917.

"Formal Opening of Duluth–Port Arthur Highway Celebrated with Large Attendance," *Cook County News Herald,* August 22, 1917.

"The Formal Opening of the Duluth–Port Arthur Highway to Be Celebrated by Proper Ceremonies," *Cook County News Herald,* August 15, 1917.

"Here's the Tale of How Rotarians Bridged a Gap Back in '17," *Cook County News Herald,* October 7, 1971; republished, *The Rotarian* magazine (June 1971).

"Pigeon River Will Get Steel Bridge," *Cook County News Herald,* July 3, 1930.

"Rotarians Will Reminisce About 'Outlaw Bridge' of 1917 When They Meet Here Saturday," *Cook County News Herald,* October 6, 1955.

Darrel and Larry Ryden, interviews conducted by Pat Zankman, n.d., Cook County Historical Society, Grand Marais, MN.

Ed and Mabel Ryden, interview, April 1, 1980, Cook County Historical Society, Grand Marais, MN.

HOVLAND DOCK

Archives, Cook County Historical Society, Grand Marais, MN.

"Matilda Tormondsen," Schroeder Area Historical Society, *Newsletter* (June 2007): 1–5.

Two Harbors, 100 Years: A Pictorial History of Two Harbors, Minnesota, and Surrounding Communities (Two Harbors, MN: Iron Ore Centennial Committee, 1984), 80–82.

NANIBOUJOU LODGE

"Duluth Group Announces Big Development," *Cook County News Herald,* November 24, 1927.

Denis Gardner, *Minnesota Treasures: Stories Behind the State's Historic Places* (St. Paul: Minnesota Historical Society Press, 2004), 266–69.

"Naniboujou Club Opened Sunday," *Cook County News Herald,* July 11, 1929.

Nancy Ramey, co-owner of Naniboujou Lodge, interview, December 2007.

ST. FRANCIS XAVIER CHURCH

Staci Drouillard, "The Village of Chippewa City," Cook County Historical Society.

Jeffrey Hess, "St. Francis Xavier Church," National Register of Historic Places registration form (July 29, 1985), State Historic Preservation Office, Minnesota Historical Society, St. Paul, MN.

George Morrison, *Turning the Feather Around: My Life in Art* (St. Paul: Minnesota Historical Society Press, 1998).

GRAND MARAIS HARBOR

Archives, Cook County Historical Society, Grand Marais, MN.

Terry Pepper, "Seeing the Light: Grand Marais Light," www.terrypepper.com/lights/superior/gdmarais-mn/index.htm.

LUTSEN AND WHITE SKY ROCK

Archives, Cook County Historical Society, Grand Marais, MN.

"Lodges of the North Shore," *Album* series (#710), WDSE-TV, Duluth, MN.

"Lutsen Mountains," www.lutsen.com.

Alta McQuatters, descendant of White Sky, interview, February 2008, Lutsen, MN.

SCHROEDER LUMBER COMPANY BUNKHOUSE

Mary T. Bell, *Cutting Across Time: Logging, Rafting and Milling the Forests of Lake Superior* (Schroeder, MN: Schroeder Area Historical Society, 1999), 6–7, 13–19, 24–26, 34–36.

Roots in the Past, Seeds for the Future: The Heritage and History of Clover Valley, French River and Surrounding Communities (Duluth, MN: Clover Valley/French River Community History Committee, North Shore Elementary School, 2000), 45–49.

J. C. Ryan, *Early Loggers in Minnesota* (Duluth: Minnesota Timber Producer's Association, 1976), 5–7.

STICKNEY STORE

Horace "Skip" Lamb, nephew of Horace Stickney, interview, November 2007.

TACONITE HARBOR

Archives, Schroeder Area Historical Society, Schroeder, MN.

Horace "Skip" Lamb, interview, November 2007.

COLONIAL DINING ROOM

Rosemary (Rudstrom) Elbert, interview, November/December 2007.

Wayne and Jennifer Frame, owners of Spirit of Gitchee Gumee/Colonial Dining Room, Little Marais, MN.

AZTEC HOTEL AND CABINOLA COURT

"Agents Celebrate 25th Anniversary in Business," *Rear View Mirror,* a publication of Northland Greyhound Lines, August 1945.

Pauline Illgen Petersen, unpublished memoir (1984), held by Bernie Young, Silver Bay, MN.

"Rudolph and Mary Illgen: Pioneers Who Saw Some of Their Dreams Come True," *Silver Bay News,* June 10, 1958.

3M AND CRYSTAL BAY

Hugh E. Bishop, *By Water and Rail: A History of Lake County Minnesota* (Two Harbors, MN: Lake County Historical Society, 2000), 59–65.

Virginia Huck, *The Brand of Tartan: The 3M Story* (New York: Appleton-Century-Crofts and Minnesota Mining and Manufacturing Co., 1955).

Two Harbors, 100 Years: A Pictorial History of Two Harbors and Surrounding Communities (Two Harbors, MN: Iron Ore Centennial Committee, 1984), 108–11.

MATTSON FISH HOUSE

1938 lake trout egg collection figures: courtesy Steve Geving, Lake Superior Area Fisheries Archives, French River Fish Hatchery, Minnesota Department of Natural Resources.

Arnold and Milford Johnson, "Commercial Fishing in Lake Superior" (speech to Two Harbors [MN] Rotary Club, March 4, 1936), Lake County Historical Society archives, Two Harbors, MN.

Matti Kaups, "North Shore Commercial Fishing, 1849–1870," *Minnesota History* 46 (Spring 1978): 42–58.

Alvera Pierson and Alvin Anderson, interview, January 2008, Duluth, MN.

Roots in the Past, Seeds for the Future: The Heritage and History of Clover Valley, French River and Surrounding Communities (Duluth, MN: Clover Valley/French River Community History Committee, North Shore Elementary School, 2000), 33–34, 36–43.

Ian Stewart, "Edward and Lisa Mattson House and Fish House," National Register of Historic Places registration form (1990), State Historic Preservation Office, Minnesota Historical Society, St. Paul, MN.

Bill Ulland, interview, January 2008.

Virginia Mattson Ulland, interview, August 2006.

SPLIT ROCK LIGHTHOUSE LENS

Connie Jo Kendall, "Let There Be Light: The History of Lighthouse Illuminants," *Clockworks* (Spring 1997): 22–32.

Terry Pepper, "Seeing the Light: Split Rock Lighthouse," www.terrypepper.com/lights/superior/splitrock/splitrock.htm.

Lee Radzak, historic site manager, Split Rock Lighthouse, interview, November/December 2007.

Thomas Tag, "The Jewel in the Sand: Manufacturing Lighthouse Lenses," *American Lighthouse* (Spring 2000): 22–27.

Information on the clockworks associated with the Split Rock Lighthouse beacon: Thomas Tag, "Report," October 21, 2002, Great Lakes Lighthouse Research, Dayton, OH.

SPLIT ROCK RIVER PILINGS

David Radford, "Report," December 2000, prepared for the Minnesota Department of Natural Resources, Division of Parks and Recreation.

Roots in the Past, Seeds for the Future: The Heritage and History of Clover Valley, French River and Surrounding Communities (Duluth, MN: Clover Valley/French River Community History Committee, North Shore Elementary School, 2000), 45–49.

SPLIT ROCK TRADING POST

Hugh E. Bishop, *By Water and Rail: A History of Lake County Minnesota* (Two Harbors, MN: Lake County Historical Society, 2000), 153–54.

Duane Sheppard, owner of Split Rock Trading Post, interview, July 2007.

GOOSEBERRY FALLS STATE PARK REFECTORY

Henry Bulter, attorney for Vilas estate, letter, July 5, 1938, regarding land deal with state of Minnesota, Gooseberry Falls State Park archives, Two Harbors, MN.

"Gooseberry Falls State Park National Register Listing," www.mnhs.org/places/nationalregister/stateparks/Gooseberry.html.

"Gooseberry Park Draws Tourists," *Duluth Herald*, September 4, 1938.

Bert Keller, CCC enrollee at Gooseberry from 1938 to 1940, interview, January 2008, Two Harbors, MN.

Minnesota State Parks and Recreation Plan (1939), State Parks Projects Files, State Archives, Minnesota Historical Society, St. Paul, MN.

TWO HARBORS LIGHTHOUSE

Dale R. Congdon, *The Light on Agate Bay: The Story of the Two Harbors Lighthouse and Its Keepers* (Two Harbors, MN: Lake County Historical Society, 2005), 18–23, 58–60, 70, 99–103, 111–14.

Denis Gardner, *Minnesota Treasures: Stories Behind the State's Historic Places* (St. Paul: Minnesota Historical Society Press, 2004), 113–15.

TWO HARBORS HIGH SCHOOL

"Dedication of New School," *Two Harbors Chronicle*, February 8, 1940.

"Four Year WPA Accomplishments," *Two Harbors Chronicle*, March 28, 1940.

Francis V. O'Connor, *Art for the Millions: Essays from the 1930s by Artists and Administrators of the WPA Federal Art Project* (Greenwich, CT: New York Graphic Society, 1973).

KENDALL'S SMOKE HOUSE

Gordy Olson and Kristi Kendall Olson, interviews, September/December 2007.

"Russ Kendall Dies at Age 85," *Duluth News Tribune*, September 4, 2007.

GARDENWOOD MOTEL AND TOURIST COURT

Dudley Elmgren, interview, December 2007, Brimson, MN.

Dan and Joy Jacobsen, owners of Gardenwood Motel and Cabin Court, interview, August 2007, Duluth, MN.

GILMORE THEATER

"About the Gilmores," program, ca. 1950, Northeast Minnesota Historical Center, University of Minnesota, Duluth.

Pat Copeland, "Island Film Colony a Vanished Dream," *Anna Maria (FL) Island Sun,* November 2004.

"Dream Theater Overlooking Lake Will Become a Reality," *Duluth News Tribune,* August 6, 1944.

"North Shore Theater Opens Monday," *Duluth Herald,* July 12, 1949.

"Summer Theater," *Duluth News Tribune,* October 24, 1948.

"Theatre 61 to Take over Former Gilmore Playhouse," *Duluth Herald,* June 14, 1957.

LESTER RIVER FISH HATCHERY

"Cradle for Finnies: The New Fish Hatchery to Be Built on Lester River by U.S. Government," *Lake Superior News,* March 12, 1887.

"The Fish Hatchery," *Lake Superior News,* August 28, 1886.

Russell W. Fridley, "Lester River Fish Hatchery," National Register of Historic Places registration form (October 6, 1977), State Historic Preservation Office, Minnesota Historical Society, St. Paul, MN.

Steve Geving, Minnesota Department of Natural Resources, French River Hatchery, interview, January 2008, Duluth, MN.

"Lester River Hatchery Is Ordered Shut," *Duluth News Tribune,* January 2, 1946.

Twelfth and Thirteenth Annual Reports of the Minnesota Commission of Fisheries, July 31, 1884, to July 31, 1886, Minnesota Historical Society, St. Paul, MN.

"The United States Fish Commission Visits Lester River on Saturday," *Lake Superior News,* December 17, 1887.

DULUTH ARMORY

Armory Arts and Music Center, proposal to the Duluth City Council, 2007.

Stephanie Hemphill, "Using the Past to Shape the Future," Minnesota Public Radio, December 10, 2001, www.minnesotapublicradio.org.

Preservation Alliance of Minnesota, "Ten Most Endangered Historic Properties," www.mnpreservation.org.

AERIAL LIFT BRIDGE

Denis Gardner, *Minnesota Treasures: Stories Behind the State's Historic Places* (St. Paul: Minnesota Historical Society Press, 2004), 107–12.

Tom Lutz, "Aerial Lift Bridge," National Register of Historic Places registration form (March 1973), State Historic Preservation Office, Minnesota Historical Society, St. Paul, MN.

Jerry Sandvick, "Stage 1: Aerial Transfer Ferry Bridge," *Nor'easter: The Journal of the Lake Superior Marine Museum Association* 30.1 (2005): 3.

ESKO'S FINNS

Esko Area Historical Society, Esko, MN.

Federal Writers' Project, *The WPA Guide to Minnesota* (St. Paul: State of Minnesota, 1938; reprint, St. Paul: Minnesota Historical Society Press, 1985), 292.

June D. Holmquist, *They Chose Minnesota: A Survey of the State's Ethnic Groups* (St. Paul: Minnesota Historical Society Press, 1981), 304.

Hans R. Wasastjema, *History of the Finns in Minnesota,* (Duluth, MN: Finnish-American Historical Society, 1957).

BARNUM CREAMERY

Archives, Carlton County Historical Society, Cloquet, MN.

Dawn Marie Eller, *Always Onward: Barnum, Minnesota— 1889 to 2002* (Barnum, MN: City of Barnum, 1988), 48–49, 80–83, 123–25, 163.

Federal Writers' Project, *The WPA Guide to Minnesota* (St. Paul: State of Minnesota, 1938; reprint, St. Paul: Minnesota Historical Society Press, 1985), 293–94.

MOOSE LAKE DEPOT

Archives, Moose Lake Area Historical Society/Fires of 1918 Museum, Moose Lake, MN.

NEMADJI "INDIAN" POTTERY

Archives, Moose Lake Area Historical Society, Moose Lake, MN.

Michelle D. Lee, *The Myth and Magic of Nemadji "Indian" Pottery: A History, Identification and Value Guide* (Moose Lake, MN: Left Hand Publishing Co., 2004), 22–29, 41–44, 94–100.

WILLOW RIVER RUTABAGA PLANT

Charles Nelson, "The Willow River Rutabaga Plant," National Register of Historic Places registration form (June 21, 1990), State Historic Preservation Office, Minnesota Historical Society, St. Paul, MN.

THE GREAT HINCKLEY FIRE

Daniel James Brown, *Under a Flaming Sky: The Great Hinckley Firestorm of 1894* (New York: Harper Perennial, 2006), 66–67, 76–79, 96–102.

Mark Haidet, "Hinckley Fire Relief House," National Register of Historic Places registration form (March 1980), State Historic Preservation Office, Minnesota Historical Society, St. Paul, MN.

Grace Stageberg Swenson, *From the Ashes: The Story of the Hinckley Fire of 1894* (Stillwater, MN: Croixside Press, 1979), 109–10, 127, 137.

TOBIE'S

Randy and Susan Hickle, owners of Tobie's, interview, December 2007.

GRANT HOUSE

Britta Bloomberg, "The Grant House Hotel," National Register of Historic Places registration form (January 1980), State Historic Preservation Office, Minnesota Historical Society, St. Paul, MN.

OLD RUSH CITY FERRY

Donna Heath, "Riverdale Ferry Is Soderbeck Legend," *Pine City Pioneer,* December 1979.

"River Ferry Crossings Along the St. Croix River," *The Dalles Visitor* 23 (summer 1991).

CARPENTER'S STEAKHOUSE

Michael and Cathy Anderson, owners of Carpenter's, interview, November 2007.

WHITE BEAR LAKE TOWNSHIP HALL

Cass Gilbert Society, www.cassgilbertsociety.org.

Paul Clifford Larson, architectural historian, interview, December 2007.

"Township Has Plans for Building Relocation, New Construction," *White Bear Press,* March 14, 2007.

"White Bear Town Hall Designed by Architect Cass Gilbert," *Town Life Magazine* (White Bear Lake, MN), 2006.

JOHNSON BOATWORKS

John W. Johnson, interview, December 2007.

John W. Johnson, *John O. Johnson: From Norway to White Bear Lake* (Decorah, IA: Anundsen Publishing, 2000), 3–6, 27–35, 51–59, 83–89.

Tom Vandervoort, former member White Bear Yacht Club, interview.

KSTP RADIO

Archives, Hubbard Broadcasting, Inc., St. Paul, MN.

Pavek Museum of Broadcasting, St. Louis Park, MN.

DAYTON'S BLUFF COMMERCIAL CLUB

Dayton's Bluff Commercial Club, "Picturesque Dayton's Bluff," pamphlet (St. Paul, MN: Jackson and Smith, 1909).

Historic Sites Survey for 770 East Seventh St., St. Paul, Ramsey County Historical Society, St. Paul, MN.

Steve Trimble, Dayton's Buff historian, interview, October 2007.

BILLY DUNN'S PLAYGROUND

"Boy, 4, Killed by Truck," *St. Paul Dispatch,* April 4, 1963.

Historic Sites Survey for 1326 Point Douglas Road, St. Paul (February 1, 1982), Ramsey County Historical Society, St. Paul, MN.

Margaret Dunn Wallner, interview, April 2007.

RED ROCK

Scott Anfinson, state archaeologist, interview, January 2008.

Kevin Callahan, "Minnesota's Red Rock and Other Sacred Boulders of the Upper Midwest" (paper read at the Society of American Archaeology conference in Chicago, IL, March 1999).

The History of Newport United Methodist Church: 1861–1974 (Newport, MN: Newport United Methodist Church, 1975).

Merrill Jarchow, "Red Rock Frontier Methodist Camp Meeting," *Minnesota History* 31 (1950): 79–89.

N. H. Winchell, *The Aborigines of Minnesota: A Report on the Collections of Jacob V. Brower and on the Field Surveys and Notes of Alfred J. Hill and Theodore H. Lewis* (St. Paul: Minnesota Historical Society, 1911).

ROCK ISLAND AND J. A. R. BRIDGE

"A Bridge Too Far Gone," *St. Paul Pioneer Press,* July 6, 2006.

Mary Charlotte Costello, *Climbing the Mississippi River Bridge by Bridge: Volume Two, Minnesota* (Cambridge, MN: Adventure Publications, 2002).

"Historic Bridge Could Get New Life," *St. Paul Pioneer Press,* May 14, 2007.

LE DUC MANSION

Wayne Gannaway, *The Le Duc Historic Site: A House of Ideals,* (South St. Paul, MN: Dakota County Historical Society, 2001), 1–3, 9–14.

RAMSEY MILL RUINS

"An Old Landmark Gone," *Hastings Gazette,* December 29, 1894.

Over the Years: Tales of a Historic Rivertown: 150 Years of Progress and Pride (South St. Paul, MN: Dakota County Historical Society, 2007), 4–5, 18–19.

"State Nominates Old Mill Park, Ruins to National Register of Historic Places," *Hastings Gazette,* September 8, 1997.

RED WING POTTERY

Archives, Goodhue County Historical Society, Red Wing, MN.

Steve Brown, Red Wing Collectors Society, interview, January 2008.

Gary and Bonnie Tefft, *Red Wing Potters and Their Wares,* 3rd ed. (Menomonee Falls, WI: Locust Enterprises, 1996), 16, 28, 96–97, 102.

SHELDON THEATRE

Sean Dowse, executive director, Sheldon Performing Arts Theatre, interview, October 2007.

Curtis Gruhl, "Sheldon Theatre," National Register of Historic Places registration form (June 3, 1979), State Historic Preservation Office, Minnesota Historical Society, St. Paul, MN.

FLORENCE TOWNSHIP HALL

"Florence Township Hall," National Register of Historic Places registration form, State Historic Preservation Office, Minnesota Historical Society, St. Paul, MN.

"Town Hall's Fate on Line," *Red Wing Republican Eagle,* March 13, 1995.

OLD FRONTENAC

Denis Gardner, *Minnesota Treasures: Stories Behind the State's Historic Places* (St. Paul: Minnesota Historical Society Press, 2004), 252–55.

Char Henn, Goodhue County Historical Society, Red Wing, MN.

Thomas Lutz, "Frontenac," National Register of Historic Places registration form (March 1973), State Historic Preservation Office, Minnesota Historical Society, St. Paul, MN.

"Our Perpetual Heritage: People, Places and Events Linked Across Yesterdays, Todays and Tomorrows," pamphlet (Florence Township Heritage Preservation Commission, 2007).

Frederick L. Smith, *The History of Frontenac* (Frontenac, MN: Methodist Campus, Inc., 1951).

FRONTENAC STONE GATES

Minnesota Department of Transportation, Historic Roadside Development Structures Inventory for "Munro Estate Gates" or "Frontenac State Park Gates," November 6, 1997.

"Nell Mabey, Noted Lake City Poet, Aided Creation of Frontenac Park," *Rochester Post-Bulletin,* August 1, 1957.

Harry Roberts, Frontenac State Park, Minnesota Department of Natural Resources, interview, November 2007.

LAKE CITY CLAMMING

Ann Barsness, "Clammers Fed the Button Industry," *Red Wing Republican Eagle,* January 1, 2000.

Char Henn, "Clamming: The Rise and Fall of an Industry" (presentation for the Goodhue County Historical Society, Red Wing, MN, 2007).

Paul Clifford Larson, "Finch's Dry Goods Store," National Register of Historic Places registration form (July 8, 1987), State Historic Preservation Office, Minnesota Historical Society, St. Paul, MN.

Rosa Larson, interview, December 2007, Pepin, Wisconsin.

Ed Storing, oral history, n.d., Wabasha County Historical Society, Reads Landing, MN.

READS LANDING

"Reads Landing," National Register of Historic Places registration form (January 1989), State Historic Preservation Office, Minnesota Historical Society, St. Paul, MN.

Wabasha County Sesquicentennial Committee, *Wabasha County* (Wabasha, MN: Wabasha County Historical Society, 1999), 29–30, 33–35.

WABASHA COUNTY POOR HOUSE

Mary DeRoos, Wabasha County Historical Society, Reads Landing, MN.

Dan Gunderson and Chris Julin, "Over the Hill to the Poor House," Minnesota Public Radio, 2002, www.minnesotapublicradio.org.

Ethel McClure, *More than a Roof: The Development of Minnesota Poor Farms and Homes for the Aged* (St. Paul: Minnesota Historical Society, 1968), 29, 78–81, 92–94, 131, 244–46.

"Wabasha County Poor House," National Register of Historic Places registration form (August 1982), State Historic Preservation Office, Minnesota Historical Society, St. Paul, MN.

ROLLINGSTONE COLONY

"Colony at Minnesota City Once Largest in the State," *Winona Republican Herald,* November 20, 1930.

History of Wabasha County: Covering Wabasha and Winona Counties (Chicago: H. H. Hill and Co., 1884).

History of Winona County—Settlement at Minnesota City, (Chicago: H. C. Cooper Jr. and Co., 1913), 149–58.

Christopher Johnson, "The Rolling Stone Colony: Labor Rhetoric in Practice," *Minnesota History* 49.4 (Winter 1984): 140–43.

Mary Nilles, Rollingstone historian, interview, 2004, Rollingstone, MN.

THE OAKS

Walt Kelly, Jr., interview, November 2007, Winona, MN.

Patrick Marek, "Growing Up at the Oaks: They Never Stopped the Music," *Winona Shopper and Post,* May 13, 1987.

WATKINS

J. R. Watkins Company, *The Open Door to Success* (Winona, MN: J. R. Watkins Company, 1928).

Watkins Family History Society, www.watkinsfhs.net.

MINNE-O-WAH CLUB

Archives, Winona County Historical Society, Winona, MN.

Frances Bowler Edstrom, "The Minne-O-Wah Club," *Winona Saturday Morning Post,* August 25, 1979.

EMIL AND THE OTTERS

"Artful Otters," *Time Magazine,* February 27, 1939.

Nicole LaChapelle, "Emil Liers: Pioneer Naturalist and Friend to Otters," *The Argus,* January/February 2004.

Emil Liers, *An Otter's Story* (New York: Viking Press, 1953).

"And Otter Things," *Saturday Evening Post,* February 14, 1942, 4.

LA CRESCENT APPLES

Donna Christoph Huegel, *Stealing the Mississippi River: Fascinating History of the La Crescent, Minnesota Area* (Bangor, WI: Joel Lovstad Publishing, 2005), 20–32.

Suggested Reading

BOOKS

Bishop, Hugh E. *By Water and Rail: A History of Lake County, Minnesota.* Duluth, MN: Lake Superior Port Cities, 2000.

Brown, Daniel James. *Under a Flaming Sky: The Great Hinckley Firestorm of 1894.* New York: Harper Perennial, 2006.

Congdon, Dale R. *The Light on Agate Bay: The Story of the Two Harbors Lighthouse and Its Keepers.* Two Harbors, MN: Lake County Historical Society, 2005.

Gardner, Denis P. *Minnesota Treasures: Stories Behind the State's Historic Places.* St. Paul: Minnesota Historical Society Press, 2004.

Huegel, Donna Christoph. *Stealing the Mississippi River: Fascinating History of the La Crescent, Minnesota Area.* Bangor, WI: Joel Lovstad Publishing, 2005.

Johnson, John W. *John O. Johnson: From Norway to White Bear Lake.* Decorah, IA: Anundsen Publishing, 2000.

Kubista, Ivan. *This Quiet Dust: A Chronicle of Old Frontenac.* New York: Vantage Press, 1978.

Lee, Michelle D. *The Myth and Magic of Nemadji "Indian" Pottery: History, Identification, and Value Guide.* Moose Lake, MN: Left Hand Publishing, 2004.

Rubenstein, Sarah P. *Minnesota History Along the Highways: A Guide to Historic Markers and Sites.* St. Paul: Minnesota Historical Society Press, 2003.

Sommer, Barbara W. *Hard Work and a Good Deal: The Civilian Conservation Corps in Minnesota.* St. Paul: Minnesota Historical Society Press, 2008.

The WPA Guide to Minnesota: The Federal Writers' Project Guide to 1930s Minnesota. 1938. Reprint, St. Paul: Minnesota Historical Society Press, 1985.

INTERNET RESOURCES

www.deadpioneer.com
An excellent website maintained by Andrew Munsch, with a wonderful page dedicated to lost Minnesota highways with special emphasis on Highway 61's original alignment south of St. Paul.

www.redwingcollectors.org
The website for the Red Wing Collectors Society. Good information on Red Wing Pottery history and events.

www.roadsideamerica.com
An "online guide to offbeat tourist attractions." Perfect for road trips.

County and local historical society websites

www.carltoncountyhistory.org

www.crossriverheritage.org

www.dakotahistory.org

www.goodhuehistory.mus.mn.us

www.lakecountyhistoricalsociety.org

www.whitebearhistory.org

www.winonahistory.org

Index

Picture Credits

pages 3, 14 (bottom), 15, 17 (top), 19, 29 (top), 43 (top and bottom), 51, 55, 61, 65 (top), 66, 68, 70 (top), 71, 81, 88 (top), 90, 92 (top), 94 (top and bottom), 98 (top), 99, 104, 106 (top), 108 (top), 115, 116, 121 Minnesota Historical Society collections

page 4 courtesy Conrad Leighton, from negative of Walter Hoffman, depot agent at Hinckley, MN, and his wife, Edna

pages 5, 18, 48, 53, 67 author's collection

page 10 Cook County Historical Society

page 20 courtesy Alta McQuatters, White Sky's granddaughter

pages 21 (top), 23 (top and bottom), 25 (top) courtesy the Lamb Family and the Schroeder Area Historical Society

pages 26, 27 courtesy Rosemary Elbert

page 31 Lake County Historical Society

page 33 from exhibition at the North Shore Commercial Fishing Museum, photographer unknown

page 38 courtesy Duane and Sharon Sheppard, St. Cloud

page 40 (top) courtesy Gooseberry Falls State Park

page 45 Gordy and Kristi (Kendall) Olson

page 50 Northeast Minnesota Historical Center, Duluth, MN, S2386B9f17 (top) and VF Gilmore Theater (bottom)

page 58 Carlton County Historical Society

page 74 White Bear Lake Area Historical Society

page 77 from John W. Johnson, *John O. Johnson: From Norway to White Bear Lake*

page 78 courtesy KSTP-AM, LLC

page 80 courtesy Steve Trimble

page 84 (top) Ramsey County Historical Society

page 86 Minnesota Annual Conference of the United Methodist Church

page 105 clamshell buckles, buttons, and blank-drilled shells from the collections of the Goodhue County Historical Society

pages 109, 111, 117, 119 (left and right) Winona County Historical Society

page 112 memorabilia courtesy Walt Kelly, photo by Denny Behr

page 118 courtesy Beth Nelson, photo by Denny Behr

All other photographs by Denny Behr

Maps by Map Hero—Matt Kania